Elizabeth Gaskell

Tessa Brodetsky

BERG *Leamington Spa*

To the memory of Paul
with whose help this book would never have been finished!

Published in 1986 by **Berg Publishers Ltd**
24 Binswood Avenue, Leamington Spa, CV32 5SQ, UK

© Tessa Brodetsky 1986

British Library Cataloguing in Publication Data

Brodetsky, Tessa
    Elizabeth Gaskell.—(Berg women's series)
    1. Gaskell, Elizabeth—Biography   2. Novelists,
    English—19th century—Biography
    I. Title
    823'.8   PR4711

    ISBN 0–907582–89–3
    ISBN 0–907582–83–4 Pbk

Library of Congress Cataloging-in-Publication Data

Brodetsky, Tessa.
    Elizabeth Gaskell.

    (Berg women's series)
    Bibliography: p.
    Includes index.
    1. Gaskell, Elizabeth Cleghorn, 1810–1865.
2. Novelists, English—19th century—Biography.
I. Title. II. Series.
PR4711.B76   1986   823'.8   86–1045
ISBN 0–907582–89–3
ISBN 0–907582–83–4 (pbk.)

Printed in Great Britain by Oxford University Press, Oxford

Further volumes in the series
General Editor: MICHAEL LOCHAN

Gertrude Bell   SUSAN GOODMAN
Mme de Staël   RENEE WINEGARTEN
Emily Dickinson   DONNA DICKENSON
Mme du Châtelet   ESTHER EHRMAN

In preparation
Anna Freud   RENEE PATON
Marie Stopes   SUSAN GOODMAN
George Sand   DONNA DICKENSON
Clara Schumann   GLENDA ABRAMSON
Simone Weil   PAT LITTLE
Emily Carr   RUTH GOWERS

Contents

Illustrations

Unless otherwise acknowledged all photographs are by the author.

The portrait of Elizabeth Gaskell on the cover is by George
   Richmond, 1851.

Introduction

Whether to entitle this book *Elizabeth Gaskell* or *Mrs Gaskell* presented something of a problem. The final decision may be seen as a tribute to her independence and strength of character; it in no way implies that she considered her primary role as other than a wife and mother, with all the duties and responsibilities this involved in mid-nineteenth century England. It is in fact of considerable interest to see how well she was able to combine her dependent position as Mrs Gaskell with her role as Elizabeth Gaskell, a writer of substantial standing among her contemporaries.

It has been a particular pleasure for me to spend time studying the life and work of Elizabeth Gaskell, and to revisit the area in which she lived. It has revived many memories, for I grew up in and knew well the Manchester and Cheshire areas which were her home for many years; I even went to school in Dover Street, where she lived when she first came to Manchester as a married woman. For the opportunity to indulge in this nostalgia, I must especially thank my editor, Miriam Kochan, and express my gratitude for the great encouragement and help she has given me.

My other great, indeed incalculable, debt is to my sister-in-law, Adèle Kitrick, who has performed the marathon task of typing (and retyping) this book, deciphering without complaint my semi-legible scrawl. She has also given me invaluable help in matters of expression and the nitty-gritty details of punctuation; any faults now remaining are entirely my responsibility.

I should also like to express my sincere appreciation to the many other friends who have kindly supported my endeavours in writing this book.

Tessa Brodetsky
Oxford, 1985

Acknowledgments

I should like to thank the staff of the Summertown Library, Oxford, and the Knutsford Library, Cheshire, for their help and courtesy in providing me with material.

I also gratefully acknowledge permission from the following to reproduce material:

Manchester University Press for the many extracts from *The Letters of Mrs Gaskell*, edited by J. A. V. Chapple and Arthur Pollard.

The National Portrait Gallery, for the portraits of Elizabeth Gaskell and of Charlotte Brontë, both by George Richmond, RA.

The City Art Gallery, Manchester for the portrait of Mrs Gaskell taken shortly before her death.

The Brontë Society, Haworth, for the photograph of Haworth Church and Parsonage, taken from Mrs Gaskell's drawing of 1857.

The Cheshire Libraries and Museums for the portrait of Mrs Gaskell by her daughter, Meta, the original of which is in the Knutsford Library.

1 A Woman of her Time

Do you not know I am a woman?
When I think, I must speak.
Shakespeare: *As You Like It*

Elizabeth Gaskell is a model *par excellence* of a mid-Victorian middle-class woman. She was a deeply caring wife and mother, inherently religious, sharing her husband's concerns as a Unitarian minister, showing an awareness and knowledge of much of rural England with its self-contained smalltown life, but also living in and very much a part of the vigorous industrial growth of an expanding city, Manchester. She used these different facets of her experience to great effect in her writing, so that from its sum total we cannot but be aware of the fabric of her life and that of the society in which she lived. Yet it seems something of an impertinence to write a biographical sketch of someone who wrote:

> I disapprove so entirely of the plan of writing "notices" or "memoirs" of living people, that I must send you on the answer I have already sent to many others; namely an entire refusal to sanction what is to me so objectionable and indelicate a practice, by furnishing a single fact with regard to myself. (L. 571)[1]

Perhaps, almost a century and a half later, she would not object to an outline of the broad sweep of her life, to help us to appreciate the reality behind her fiction. She does in any case refer specifically to *living* people, and indeed she herself, at the request of Charlotte Brontë's father, felt she was giving something of interest and value to the world in her biography of Charlotte.

Elizabeth Cleghorn Stevenson was born in London in 1810. Her father, who was from Berwick-on-Tweed, came from a seafaring family, whilst her mother's family, the Hollands, with whom she always had a very close connection, were natives of

1

Cheshire, many of them involved in farming, and very much a part of the rural way of life. Both these influences, the naval and the rural, are evident in many of the settings and characters we find in Mrs Gaskell's stories. She was the youngest of eight children, but she and her brother John, the eldest, were the only ones to survive infancy. He was twelve years older than Elizabeth, and little is known of his life. When he was twenty-one he went to sea, and after that was mostly out of England until he finally disappeared on a voyage to India in 1828. A number of characters in the novels are sailors, for example Will Wilson in *Mary Barton*, Frederick Hale in *North and South*, and Charlie Kinraid in *Sylvia's Lovers*. It seems clear that the idea of the young man who goes to sea stimulated her imagination, and such characters are portrayed as brave, daring even to the point of recklessness, and possessing an attractive sparkle. She appears to have remembered her brother with affection, and she wrote of the brother–sister relationship as a close and loving one.

Her mother died when she was only thirteen months old, and she was brought up by her mother's sister, 'darling Aunt Lumb', in Knutsford, which was to become known to readers as Cranford, and as Hollingford in *Wives and Daughters*. Her life there gave her a deep love for, and an intimate knowledge of, rural scenes and life, and this forms the basis of many fine descriptive passages, which show acute, detailed observation and appreciation of the natural world:

> The hill fell suddenly down into the plain, extending for a dozen miles or more. There was a clump of dark Scotch firs close to them, which cut clear against the western sky, and threw back the nearest levels into distance. The plain below them was richly wooded, and was tinted by the young tender hues of the earliest summer, for all the trees of the wood had donned their leaves except the cautious ash, which here and there gave a soft, pleasant greyness to the landscape. Far away in the champaign were spires, and towers, and stacks of chimneys belonging to some distant hidden farmhouse, which were traced downwards through the golden air by the thin columns of blue smoke sent up from the evening fires. The view was bounded by some rising ground in deep purple shadow against the sunset sky. (*Ruth*, p. 52)

Elizabeth Gaskell, from a watercolour portrait by her daughter Meta

(*overleaf, top*)
93 Cheyne Walk, Chelsea, the birthplace of Elizabeth Stevenson
(*at foot*)
Heathside, Knutsford, where Elizabeth Stevenson grew up. The house is
now known as Heathwaite House

Her father remained in London and remarried three years after his first wife died. From time to time Elizabeth visited him, her stepmother and the two children of that marriage, but she does not appear to have enjoyed this; indeed, she herself wrote in later life: 'Long ago I lived in Chelsea occasionally with my father and step-mother, and *very, very* unhappy I used to be'. (L. 616) However, she obviously benefited academically from her father's teaching; during a longer period she spent with him, he tutored her in Latin, French and Italian, and her proficiency is evident in much of her writing.

Long before this, however, at the age of twelve, she left Knutsford to go to a school, Avonbank, in Warwickshire, run by the Byerley sisters. She enjoyed her school-days, and was obviously treated with kindness, as well as receiving an education which encouraged her to read widely, and to adopt an understanding, liberal attitude to her world. Perhaps her pleasure in her own school-days made her especially indignant at the treatment which Charlotte Brontë received when she attended the school which is immortalised as Lowood in *Jane Eyre*, and which Mrs Gaskell was to attack in her *Life of Charlotte Brontë*, thereby involving herself in considerable controversy. It is curious that a woman who in so many ways appears to have been at the centre of a loving, conventional, placid family, so frequently caused a storm by her writing, often to her own great surprise. Another example of this occurred in her apparent siding with the working-class *Mary Barton*, but she defended herself by explaining that:

> I can only say I wanted to represent the subject in the light in which some of the workmen certainly consider to be *true*, not that I dare to say that it is the abstract absolute truth.
>
> That some of the men do view the subject in the way I have tried to represent, I have personal evidence; and I think somewhere in the first volume you may find a sentence stating that my intention was simply to represent the view many of the work-people take. (L. 36)

A further example was in the subject matter of *Ruth*, which dealt with the plight of the fallen woman, considered by many to be an unsuitable subject for fiction, and the book was banned in many homes, including her own! 'Of course it is a prohibited book in *this*, as in many other households; not a book for young people, unless read with someone older. (I mean to read it with MA [her daughter Marianne] some quiet time or other).' (L. 148)

To return to her own life, she did not remain for long in Knutsford after she finished school, but lived in London, Newcastle and Edinburgh, staying with various relations of her mother's. In 1831 she went to Manchester to stay with a member of one of these families, Mary Robberds, whose husband was the minister of the Unitarian Cross Street chapel. At their house she met his assistant, William Gaskell. They became engaged, a match thoroughly approved of by both families, and in the following year William Gaskell and Elizabeth Cleghorn Stevenson were married in Knutsford. After a honeymoon in Wales they settled in Manchester. A hundred and fifty years later William Gaskell seems a shadowy figure, remembered chiefly as the husband of the writer, Mrs Gaskell; but in fact, in the Manchester of that period, he held a position of considerable importance, exemplified by the fact that a thousand people gathered at Manchester town hall in his honour, to celebrate the fiftieth anniversary of his appointment to the Cross Street chapel. Both William Gaskell and Elizabeth Stevenson came from Unitarian families, and to understand the outlook of the Gaskells it is necessary to realise the importance of Unitarianism at that time:

> It was an undogmatic faith with a great intellectual appeal, and a strong philanthropic and humanitarian tradition of practical activity. It had many attractions for the rising business classes of Manchester. Cross Street Chapel, in the centre of the city, adjoined the offices of the *Manchester Guardian*, and until the coming of the University this area was the intellectual hub of Manchester. Gaskell worked here for fifty-six years. Half· of the time he was the junior minister, half, the chief minister. He was at the end not only the most eminent Unitarian minister in Manchester, but also in the whole country.[2]

In addition to his work as a minister, William Gaskell lectured at local colleges in many subjects including classics, theology, English literature, local dialect and even chemistry. He was a member of many committees which were involved in philanthropic work, and he was much concerned in efforts to improve the living conditions and education of the poor amongst whom he worked.

Their family soon began to grow, but it was not without the heartache so common in that period; the first child was still-born. She was followed by three daughters, Marianne, Margaret Emily (always known as Meta) and Florence (Flossy), who thrived. Mr and Mrs Gaskell were then delighted by the birth of a son who died from scarlet fever when he was less than a year old, a loss from which his mother never fully recovered. However, perhaps her readers have benefited, partly because she started to write in a systematic way as a distraction from her grief, but especially because she was to draw on the experience of profoundly-felt sorrow in many of her novels, and to write of it with great perception and sympathy. A fourth daughter, Julia, followed and completed the family, which was a constant source of loving concern and happiness to her. In 1837, two months after the birth of her second daughter, Meta, Mrs Gaskell was deeply saddened by the death of her Aunt Lumb who had brought her up: 'Oh there never will be one like her', she wrote. (L. 5)

Her life in Manchester was a busy one, partly as a conscientious, tireless, domesticated woman, always concerned, as is evident from her letters, with the many problems and complications of running a household in the mid-nineteenth century. She was constantly involved with the welfare and education of her daughters, but no concern, however small, was beneath her notice, whether it were training a servant, trimming a new bonnet or deciding which flowers to plant in the garden. In addition, the Gaskell's house was a centre of hospitality, and frequently saw an influx of visitors. As her literary reputation grew, so did her circle of friends, and she was to entertain Charlotte Brontë, Charles Dickens, Thomas Carlyle and many other well-known Victorian figures. There is some evidence that she did not find her husband an easy man; he was frequently out in connection with various aspects of his work, and when at home tended to shut himself away in his study. There is, however, no suggestion that he did not participate in family life or take a keen interest in his wife and daughters. In fact, Mrs Gaskell was most shocked to discover that Mr Brontë never took dinner with his family after his wife died, even when Charlotte was his only remaining child — a situation which would have been totally alien to the Gaskell household: 'Fancy it! and only they two left', she wrote. (L. 166)

However, Mr Gaskell rarely accompanied his wife and daughters on their various travels, in spite of the fact that Mrs Gaskell was frequently away for long periods, especially as the girls grew older. Mr Gaskell preferred to go away on his own: to 'bachelorize off comfortably' (L. 192), and he was encouraged to do so by his wife, who was always concerned about his health and welfare: 'The "worry" relates to the congregation & I must try & arrange matters without passing the "worry" on to Papa'. (L. 198b) Her concern for him eventually involved her in buying, without his knowledge, a house in Alton, Hampshire, which was intended for his retirement, a plan which unhappily never came to fruition.

Mrs Gaskell was deeply affected by the crushing poverty and degrading conditions which were the lot of many of her fellow-citizens of Manchester. The fundamental changes in agriculture during the eighteenth century had so worsened the position of the agricultural labourers that many of them, seeing a bleak future in the country, turned to the apparently thriving towns, where the advances of the Industrial Revolution were creating rapid growth in factories, and the elusive promise of jobs and security. In the first half of the nineteenth century the population of the major industrial cities increased dramatically, due to a slight increase in the birth-rate, a fall in the death-rate after 1790 and a steady influx from the rural areas. One result of this was to worsen and intensify the already appalling housing conditions of the very poor, so that around the factories there were to be found small unpaved courts surrounded by tiny dwellings without sanitation, dark, gloomy and evil-smelling. Elizabeth Gaskell drew on her knowledge of these miserable conditions in her writing, especially in *Mary Barton* and *North and South*, and it is clear that she devoted time and effort to relieving some of the suffering which she regularly witnessed in her position as the wife of a minister.

Her time and energy seem unbounded. In addition to her loving attention to the needs of her family, to her duties as a most hospitable hostess and to her constant interest in, and work for, those in need, she found time to travel frequently and widely, and also to write copiously, not only full-length novels, short stories and her well-known biography, but also many letters, often long and full of impressive attention to the interests of her correspondents, as well as accounts of many of her own activities and thoughts and of the places she visited.

However, before considering her substantial literary output, let us turn briefly to the periods she spent away from Manchester, which were obviously essential for her mental as well as physical well-being, and were also frequently undertaken for the health of her daughters. Silverdale in Lancashire and the Lake District were favourite contrasts to 'a town with no grace or beauty in it', (L. 51) where 'one sees little or nothing of spring flowers'. (L. 617) She was anxious 'that our children learn country interests, and ways of living and thinking'. (L. 72) As the children grew up and as she became an acknowledged writer, her travels took her to many other places, including London, Oxford, Haworth and Whitby in this country, and visits, often lengthy, to Germany, Belgium, Switzerland, Italy and France. The main significance of this for her readers is that she came into contact with a wide variety of scenes and, more importantly, of people, and this resulted in an ever-increasing awareness of the many facets of human nature and of the complexity of relationships. This diversity made a profound impression on a woman of her sensitivity and acute powers of observation, and both broadened the base and enriched the texture of her work, which reached its pinnacle in her last novel, *Wives and Daughters*.

In 1845 Elizabeth Gaskell started work on her first novel, *Mary Barton*. At this time she had published only two minor pieces: an account of a visit made while at school to Clopton House, near Stratford, which was published by William Howitt in *Visits to Remarkable Places* in 1840, and a poem written in collaboration with her husband. She was encouraged to write at greater length in the first place by the Howitts, who were most impressed by her 'powerful and graphic manner of writing', and with whom she established a lasting friendship after meeting them in Heidelberg in 1841. (They were, in fact, also responsible for publishing a few of her short stories prior to the publication of *Mary Barton*.) Her husband also encouraged and supported her in writing more seriously and at greater length, especially after the death of their son in August 1845. However, from the sheer volume of her work in the last twenty years of her life, and the considerable literary merit of so much of it, one must assume that she would eventually have turned to writing, even without the external stimulus and encouragement. The subject matter of *Mary Barton* sprang directly from its author's own knowledge and experiences of the lives of the very poor and most disadvantaged in Manchester. It was one of the earliest 'social novels', for until this time the exploration of social problems had hardly been considered a suitable subject for polite conversation, let alone for fiction. In spite of a certain amount of controversy which arose after its publication in 1848, the book met with considerable acclaim, not only because of the forthright manner in which the writer exposed the appalling conditions endured by so many of her contemporaries, but also because of her obvious powers of writing a gripping story and of portraying characters with convincing depth. At first the identity of the author was unknown (she published it under the pseudonym of Cotton Mather Mills), but this did not last long, and Mrs Gaskell's recognition as an author of literary merit came in 1849, when she visited London, and was entertained at one of Samuel Rogers's famous breakfasts, in itself a recognition that she had made her mark on contemporary literature. During this visit she also met the Dickenses, the Carlyles and John Forster, with all of whom she maintained lasting friendships.

Her meeting with Dickens led to his request for her to contribute to the magazine *Household Words*, which he was just launching, and the short stories which she wrote during the next couple of years were for the most part published in it. But perhaps her most significant contribution to *Household Words* started in December 1851, and was published at erratic intervals over the following seventeen months; this was *Cranford*, her best-known and probably best-loved story. Each section, as it was published in serial form, was greeted with great enthusiasm and had many contemporary admirers, including especially Charles Dickens. There is no narrative unity, but it stands as a series of delightful insights into the life of Cranford and its inhabitants. Based on Elizabeth Gaskell's own knowledge of, and love for, Knutsford, it is written with delicate humour and sensitivity, and it alone would establish her position amongst the authors of that period.

Her next full-length novel, *Ruth*, published at the beginning of 1853, has already been referred to, because of the controversy aroused by the eponymous heroine who allowed her passions to overcome her morals, thus becoming that anathema to Victorian ideas of uprightness, the Fallen Woman. The character, Ruth, is dealt with sympathetically and sensitively by her author and, although it is not one of her best works, there are some moving scenes and much fine description. Many of her well-known contemporaries approved wholeheartedly of the book. These included Elizabeth Barrett Browning, George Eliot and Charlotte Brontë, who felt that it was unnecessary for Ruth to die, since she had suffered enough for her behaviour in her life-time: 'Why should she die? Why are we to shut the book weeping?' she wrote to Mrs Gaskell in April 1852.

1854 saw the publication in serial form of her next novel, *North and South* which, like *Mary Barton*, dealt largely with problems connected with industrialisation. The very title suggests that the author drew on her knowledge of the two contrasting environments, rural and urban industrial, with which she was so familiar. So we find the heroine, Margaret Hale, coming from the lush, rural South to the harsh, often cruel environment of Milton Northern (Manchester), peopled by those with different background, approach and outlook from the family and friends amongst whom she grew up. The story is largely concerned with her development, leading to her eventual understanding of the industrial North and those reared in it, and also with the parallel development of John Thornton, a Milton manufacturer, who was as sceptical at first of Margaret's attitudes and those of southerners in general as she was of his. This novel deals with the attitude of the manufacturer more fully and more sympathetically than did *Mary Barton*, and so did not meet with the hostile response of the earlier novel.

In 1855 her dear friend Charlotte Brontë, whom she first met in the summer of 1850, died suddenly and unexpectedly at the age of thirty-eight. Within two months Mr Brontë asked her to write a life of his daughter, and was apparently supported in this by Charlotte's husband, Mr Nicholls. It is clear that Elizabeth Gaskell was very ready to pay this tribute to someone she admired both as a novelist and as a woman who had suffered deeply but uncomplainingly. Her definitive biography paints a deeply moving and understanding picture of the lonely, isolated, tragic life led by Charlotte Brontë, so different from that of her biographer. In some ways it comes as a surprise that these two women, from such different milieux, should have formed a close relationship of great significance to both of them. The effort involved in writing this book exhausted Mrs Gaskell, and she left England for a necessary two-months' holiday, unaware of the storm which followed the publication of the only biography she was to write.

Several of her full-length novels are relatively unknown, and she has made an even smaller impact as a writer of short stories, of which she wrote quite a number during the last twenty years or so of her life. They were often written to fulfil her obligations to such publications as *Household Words*, and very often with the express intention of raising money for some special purpose, usually foreign travel. It is not surprising, therefore, that the stories are of mixed literary worth. A very few, particularly *Lois the Witch* and *Cousin Phillis*, stand on their own merit, but many are interesting mainly for the way in which they deal with themes that she developed more fully and more maturely in her full-length novels; for example *Lizzie Leigh*, which deals with the plight of the unmarried mother.

It was during her stay in Rome after finishing the biography of Charlotte Brontë that Mrs Gaskell met Charles Eliot Norton, with whom she formed a friendship of great importance to them both. He was much younger than she was — just thirty, whereas she was forty-six. The weeks spent in Rome had a magical quality for her: 'It was in those charming Roman days that my life, at any rate, culminated. I shall never be so happy again. I don't think I was ever so happy before', she wrote in 1857. (L. 375) Norton was a young American, who at the time he met Elizabeth Gaskell was travelling in Europe and soaking up European culture. Before returning to the States he spent a week with the Gaskells in Manchester. After that, he and Elizabeth Gaskell kept up a regular correspondence ranging widely over a great variety of topics, including the trivia of daily household events and family news, references to matters contemporary concern and, occasionally, to her writing. These letters provide a very valuable insight into the texture of Mrs Gaskell's life and interests.

Her next major work was *Sylvia's Lovers*, set in Monkshaven (Whitby) during the Napoleonic wars. The exploits of the press-gangs are depicted, especially the effect of the seizures on the families and friends of those taken. This novel, of which Mrs Gaskell said: 'It is the saddest story I ever wrote', is concerned with the problems, misunderstandings and irrational behaviour often occasioned by love. Overall it has a number of weaknesses, but it also contains much fine description and some delightful character cameos.

Mrs Gaskell's final novel, of which the last chapter was unfinished when she died in 1865, was *Wives and Daughters*. It is a story of relationships, primarily between Dr Gibson, his daughter Molly, his second wife and her daughter Cynthia Kirkpatrick, and between all of these and the local Squire's family, the Hamleys. It presents a delightful picture of smalltown life, its prejudices and snobberies, and also its caring and concern for individuals. It is told with delicate irony and humour, and contains many fine character sketches. Both in subject-matter and in the light, sure touch of the writing, it is reminiscent of Jane Austen, and stands as the culmination of Mrs Gaskell's creative genius.

She found the writing of *Wives and Daughters*, which took about eighteen months, exhausting, and she was often ill during this period. She spent much time away from home as the climate in Manchester exacerbated her own health problems and these, together with her concern about those of her husband, no doubt influenced the project with which she was involved. This was the purchase of the house in Alton, Hampshire. As she wrote to Charles Eliot Norton:

> And then I did a terribly grand thing! and a secret thing too! only you are in America and can't tell. I bought a house and 4 acres of land in Hampshire, — near Alton, — for Mr Gaskell to retire to and for a home for my unmarried daughters. (L. 583)

By this time Florence was married and Marianne engaged, but Meta and Julia never married. The house was called 'The Lawn', and she bought it probably in July 1865, although not intending to move there permanently for several years. In November she was staying there with several members of the family when, as Meta wrote in a letter in January 1866:

> He [Charlie Crompton, Florence's husband] and I had been a walk on the Sunday afternoon. But Mama, Florence, and Julia had been to church – and the clergyman had noticed how particularly well Mama was looking. Then we had all come in, and we had tea, and then were sitting around the fire in the drawingroom, so cozily and happily – (darling Mama talking

and planning a most kind plan of lending the house to Lady Crompton who was very much broken down) – when *quite* suddenly, without a moment's warning, in the midst of a sentence, she fell forwards – dead.[3]

Mrs Gaskell was buried in the grounds of the Brook Street Unitarian chapel in her beloved Knutsford. William Gaskell never moved from Manchester, but continued as Unitarian Minister at the Cross Street chapel until his death in 1884; he went on living in the family home at 42 (now 84) Plymouth Grove, and Julia and Meta also remained there until they died.

Elizabeth Cleghorn Gaskell emerges as a woman of great energy and many interests, the foremost being the welfare of her family. She was also much concerned about the people of Manchester amongst whom she lived and worked; we see through her writing a clear picture of a woman who was gentle, sympathetic, understanding, full of humour, and of a charming simplicity which was never marred by her considerable literary reputation. She was a woman who did not hesitate to expose the evils of her world when she encountered them, but who accepted the values of that world, and exemplified many of its fundamental attitudes and beliefs, especially the paramount importance of the family, of religion and of the duties, responsibilities and compassion expected of the more fortunate in society.

Notes

1. Here, as in the following references, the figure denotes the number of the letter (L.) as listed in *The Letters of Mrs Gaskell*, ed. A. Pollard and J. A. V. Chapple, Manchester UP, Manchester, 1966.
2. John Levitt, 'William Gaskell and the Lancashire Dialect', *Journal of the Lancashire Dialect Society*, no. 31 (1982), p. 36.
3. A. B. Hopkins, *Elizabeth Gaskell, Her Life and Work*, John Lehmann, London, 1952, p. 319.

2 The Industrial Scene — First Reactions: *Mary Barton*

> You may tempt the upper classes
> With your villainous demi-tasses,
> But Heaven will protect the Working Girl.
> Edgar Smith (1857–1938)

Disraeli's novel, *Sybil*, subtitled *The Two Nations*, was published in 1845. It deals with what came to be known as 'the condition of England question', and in it he describes the lives of the working-classes of the period. The two nations of the title are the rich and the poor, and *Mary Barton*, Mrs Gaskell's first novel, is dominated by the same theme, the separateness of rich and poor. These early social novels derived their main force from the exposure of the social problems dividing the nation. Other novels in this genre written during the same period include *Coningsby* by Disraeli, *Yeast* and *Alton Locke* by Charles Kingsley, and many of Dickens's novels (in whole or in part), perhaps most memorably *Oliver Twist*, *Bleak House* and *Hard Times*.

The revolution in agriculture during the last half of the eighteenth century brought about the enclosure of open fields and commons. The larger farms thus created, together with improved, more scientific methods of farming, resulted in much greater yields of crops, especially corn; during the French wars, from 1793 to 1815, farmers, encouraged to produced food for the nation, enjoyed great prosperity, for there was a ready market for all the corn they could produce. However, the majority of small landholders and cottars lost what living they previously had from the land, and either worked for the large landowners for low wages, or wandered into the expanding industrial towns in search of work and a higher standard of living. In the main, however, they were disappointed, for in the towns there was much unemployment, especially as many women and children were employed in the factories and mills for long hours and very low wages, thus providing a supply of much cheaper labour than the

13

men did. The desperate shortage of work, and therefore of money, led to a great deal of unrest, culminating in such events as the Peterloo Massacre of 1819 in Manchester. A large crowd had assembled in St Peter's Field in Manchester to listen to a well-known radical speaker, 'Orator' Henry Hunt, but the local magistrates, fearing a riot, sent in mounted yeomanry to arrest Hunt. The yeomanry charged the crowd with sabres and, as a result, eleven people were killed and over four hundred injured. Four days after Peterloo, *The Times* published the following:

> The more attentively we have considered the relations subsisting between the upper and the labouring classes throughout some of the manufacturing districts, the more painful and unfavourable is the construction which we are forced to put upon the events of last Monday. . . . The two great divisions of society there, are — the masters, who have reduced the rate of wages; and the workmen, who complain of their masters for having done so. Turn the subject as we please, 'to this complexion it must come at last'.[1]

In 1815, at the end of the war with France, the price of corn fell and, to protect the farmers, the government passed the first Corn Law. This (followed by another in 1828) protected the income of the English farmer by prohibiting the import of corn until home-produced corn cost eighty shillings a quarter. This exacerbated the difficulties of the poor, for it resulted in much dearer flour and bread, and led to a long campaign for the repeal of the Corn Laws. This campaign reached a climax as living conditions worsened during the decade which came to be known as 'the hungry forties', and in 1845 the Corn Laws were finally repealed after occasioning much hardship and bitterness.

The unrest caused by hunger, lack of work and appalling living conditions among so many of the workers found other outlets also, one of the most important being the Chartist movement. Whereas the mainspring of the Anti-Corn Law League was economic, the Chartist movement was in addition motivated by political aims. In 1832 the first of the great Parliamentary Reform Acts had been passed, and had done much to lessen the inequalities of the political system and to introduce greater democracy into parliamentary representation. However, there was still a long way to go, and a number of politically-conscious groups, strengthened by the discontent and frustration of many working men, because their plight was largely ignored by the politicians, joined together to form the Chartist movement. In 1838 a 'People's Charter' was drawn up. There were six points embodied in it, all concerned with the reform of the parliamentary system: universal male suffrage, equal electoral districts, the removal of the property qualification for members of parliament, payment of MPs, a secret ballot and annual general elections. In 1839 delegates from all over the country converged on the House of Commons to present a petition putting forward the six points. The point of the march and the National Chartist Convention, as it was known, was confused in the minds of many, who saw it as a means of informing members of parliament of the dismal facts of their situation. They were sure this would result in an immediate amelioration of their condition, and therefore, when the House of Commons refused to accept the petition, the disappointment was more intense than a rejection of the political demands alone would have occasioned. An important episode in the novel *Mary Barton* deals with the hopes aroused by the presentation of the petition, and the effects of its rejection.

It is against this background of social discontent and deprivation, of disappointment and failure, that *Mary Barton* is set:

The whole tale grew up in my mind as imperceptibly as a seed germinates in the earth, so I cannot trace back now why or how such a thing was written, or such a character or circumstance introduced,

wrote Mrs Gaskell. She went on to say that:

'John Barton' was the original title of the book. Round the character of John Barton all the others formed themselves; he was my hero, *the* person with whom all my sympathies went, with whom I tried to identify myself at the time, because I believed from personal observation that such men were not uncommon, and would well reward such sympathy and love as should throw light down upon their groping search after the causes of suffering, and the reason why suffering is sent, and what they can do to lighten it. (L. 42)

15

It was apparently due to pressure from the publishers that the title was changed to *Mary Barton*, with the subtitle *A Tale of Manchester Life*.

The change of title alters the emphasis from that originally intended by the author, for while John's main driving force, his raison d'être, centres round the struggle between the rich and the poor, between masters and workers, which is central to the book, Mary is only marginally involved in this:

> . . .but it was hardly likely that a girl of Mary's age (even when two or three years had elapsed since her mother's death) should care much for the differences between the employers and the employed. . . (p. 59)

The struggle obviously impinges on her, both in her relationship with her father and in the contrast between the circumstances and attitudes of her two lovers, Harry Carson, the son of a prosperous mill-owner, and Jem Wilson, a mechanic from a poor background similar to Mary's. However, she does come increasingly to dominate the action, so it can be argued that the change of title was reasonable, and it was obviously considered a more attractive one.

The story is concerned with the terrible problems experienced by the working-classes during the period around 1840. It starts happily enough, with a holiday outing by the Barton and Wilson families to a favourite spot of Mrs Gaskell's, Green Heys Fields; both men are in work and they are able to live reasonably well. When they all return to the Bartons' house for tea, we learn that the room was 'warm and glowing light in every corner', and that 'Mrs Barton was proud of her crockery and glass' (p. 49). There is money enough to buy in extra food for the guests, and Mary is sent for eggs, milk, a loaf, some rum and a pound of ham, but John Barton calls to his wife: 'Say two pounds, missis, and don't be stingy' (p. 50). But we already have an indication of the vehement concern John Barton has for the problems of the poor:

> If I am out of work for weeks in the bad times, and winter comes, with black frost, and keen east wind, and there is no coal for the grate, and no clothes for the bed, and the thin bones are seen through the ragged clothes, does the rich man share his plenty

with me, as he ought to do, if his religion was not a humbug?. . . Don't think to come over me with the old tale, that the rich know nothing of the trials of the poor. I say, if they don't know, they ought to know. (p. 45)

The happiness of the first two chapters is soon destroyed; the Bartons suffer first, as during the following night Mrs Barton dies in labour:

One of the good influences over John Barton's life had departed that night. One of the ties which bound him down to the gentle humanities of earth was loosened, and henceforward the neighbours all remarked he was a changed man. His gloom and his sternness became habitual instead of occasional. He was more obstinate. (p. 58)

It is not long before the Wilsons also suffer. George Wilson loses his job after a fire in Carsons' mill where he worked, and then their twin babies die. Shortly afterwards George Wilson also dies suddenly, so that the only remaining members of the two families are Mrs Wilson and Jem on the one hand, and John Barton and Mary on the other.

Mary, who is apprenticed to a dressmaker, is flattered by the attentions of wealthy young Harry Carson, and unrealistically imagines a future as his wife, with her father living with them in ease and luxury. The parallel between her and her aunt Esther, who has disappeared from home and (after having been seduced and then abandoned) has become a streetwalker, is made evident, and even John is worried by: ' . . . this terrible superstitious fear suggested by her likeness to Esther. . .' (p. 172)

Eventually Mary is brought face to face with the choice before her, for she receives a proposal from Jem, which she rejects, and which leads to his passionate outburst:

'Mary! you'll hear, may be, of me as a drunkard, and may be as a thief, and may be as a murderer. Remember! when all are speaking ill of me, you will have no right to blame me, for it's your cruelty will have made me what I feel I shall become.' (p. 175)

No sooner has Jem left than Mary realises she has made a terrible

17

mistake and determines to avoid Harry Carson. Eventually, though, she meets him again and is confronted by the folly of her misguided daydreams: Harry Carson, frustrated by her refusal to have any more to do with him, says:

> 'I thought we could be happy enough without marriage. . . . But now, if you like, I'll get a licence to-morrow morning — nay, to-night, and I'll marry you in defiance of all the world, rather than give you up.' (p. 183)

In the meantime John has become more embittered about the situation of the poor and his inability to do anything to alter it. He has been to London as a member of the Chartist delegation of 1839 to present a petition to parliament, and is shattered by its reception:

> 'As long as I live, our rejection that day will bide in my heart; and as long as I live I shall curse them as so cruelly refused to hear us; but I'll not speak of it no more.' (pp. 144–5)

His views turn even more extreme, and he becomes involved in a plot to assassinate young Carson, whose cynical disregard of their desperate condition has infuriated the men. When Harry Carson is found murdered, his father, grief-stricken, offers a large reward to have the murderer found and brought to the gallows. Suspicion quickly falls on Jem, who is arrested and taken to Liverpool for trial.

Meanwhile, John Barton has left Manchester on a trade union delegation, unaware that his action has endangered Jem's life, or of Mary's entanglement with Harry Carson, which is now public knowledge. Mary determines to save Jem. Her situation is especially fraught when she finds evidence which reveals to her that her father is in fact the murderer. After a dramatic chase in a rowing-boat, Jem's cousin, who can provide him with an alibi, is found; he arrives at the trial at the critical moment, and Jem is found not guilty.

Mary, after a nervous collapse, returns home to find her father a broken man:

And as for his face it was sunk and worn, — like a skull, with yet a suffering expression that skulls have not! Your heart would have ached to have seen the man, however hardly you might have judged his crime. (p. 422)

After several harrowing days, John brings together Mary, Jem, an old friend Job Legh, and Mr Carson, and confesses his guilt. Mr Carson refuses to show mercy, but in a passionate speech describes his feelings for his son, and John sees him for the first time as a brother rather than an employer, and cries out: 'I did not know what I was doing.' (p. 436) This has a profound effect on Mr Carson, and he returns to the Bartons' home the next morning, where in a melodramatic scene he holds John Barton in his arms in forgiveness , as John dies. Jem now decides to emigrate to Canada with Mary and his mother, and we finally see them living in a pleasant home with a garden and orchard, with Jem and Mary's baby son.

This narrative outline can give only a superficial impression of the forceful exposure of the living conditions of the poor, of the contrast between their lives and those of the employers, and of the near inability of human beings to understand one another and enter into each other's feelings, which are the underlying themes of the book. It is also important to consider the wealth of character-drawing, and the vivid detail which brings the descriptive passages to life.

The intimate knowledge Mrs Gaskell had of the lives of the poorest of her fellow citizens must have been fermenting in her mind from the time she married and settled in Manchester in 1832. The impact this knowledge had made found a release in the mid-1840s in *Mary Barton*, and the very fact that it had been latent for so long must have increased the passion with which she exposed the appalling conditions. The contrast between the living conditions of the rich and the poor is explicitly described again and again:

At all times it is a bewildering thing to the poor weaver to see his employer removing from house to house, each one grander than the last, till he ends in building one more magnificent than all, or withdraws his money from the concern, or sells his mill to buy an estate in the country, while all the time the weaver, who thinks he and his fellows are the real makers of this wealth, is struggling on for bread for their children, through the vicissitudes of lowered wages, short hours, fewer hands employed. . . (p. 59)

The difference between the homes of the poor and that of the Carsons helps to highlight to contrast. There is a vivid description of Ben Davenport's home. He used to work with George Wilson at Carsons' mill, and also lost his job when the mill burnt down. He contracts a fever, and George Wilson enlists the support of John Barton to help the Davenport family. As they approach his home:

> . . .women from their doors tossed household slops of *every* description into the gutter; they ran into the next pool, which overflowed and stagnated. Heaps of ashes were the stepping-stones, on which the passer-by, who cared in the least for cleanliness, took care not to put his foot. (p. 98)

The Davenports live in a small cellar, which is made even darker by the rags stuffed into the gaps in the broken windows to keep out the cold air; the room stinks, and the men find:

> . . . three or four little children rolling on the damp, nay wet, brick floor, through which the stagnant, filthy moisture of the street oozed up; the fire-place was empty and black. . . (p. 98)

The two friends provide the family with what little food and comfort they can, and relieve Mrs Davenport by watching over her delirious husband during the night. This gives John Barton an opportunity to expound his ideas on the contrast between the lives of the rich and those of the poor: '"Han they ever seen a child o' their'n die for want o' food?"' (p. 105) In the morning Wilson goes to Mr Carson's home to ask for any infirmary order for Ben Davenport, an order which had to be obtained from the employer to enable a workman to have hospital treatment: 'Mr Carson's was a good house, and furnished with disregard to expense.' (p. 105) The brightness of the kitchen with its 'glittering tins' and 'roaring fire' greets Wilson, who has come straight from the dank, foetid home of the Davenports. He is ushered into the dining-room, where he finds Mr Carson and his son at 'the

empathise with him, as he has been shown to do earlier with the knob-stick. The passage is over-written and sentimental, but the underlying theme, that occasionally the gap can be bridged, is of great importance. Towards the end of the same chapter (Chapter 35) Mr Carson also bridges the gap in an equally sentimental and melodramatic passage. John Barton's cry: 'I did not know what I was doing', is taken up in an incident that Mr Carson witnesses, in which a little girl is knocked to the pavement by a careless, rough lad, but pleads with her nurse not to call a policeman: '"*He did not know what he was doing*, did you, little boy?"' (p. 438) A chord is struck in Mr Carson's mind; he goes home to his Bible and finds the sentence: 'They know not what they do'. He returns the following evening to John Barton's death-bed to pray:

'God be merciful to us sinners. — Forgive us our trespasses as we forgive them that trespass against us.'
    And when the words were said, John Barton lay a corpse in Mr Carson's arms. (pp. 441–2)

He has managed to feel for and with John Barton, if only briefly.

It is interesting that some of the most vivid character-drawing in *Mary Barton* depicts older people, who remember poignantly scenes from the past; Alice Wilson and Job Legh are two outstanding examples, neither of them central to the story, but each embodying sturdy, solid characteristics and attitudes, so obviously approved by Mrs Gaskell. Alice is a washerwoman, but also a devoted and skilful sicknurse, always ready to help her neighbours, even sitting up all night with an ill child; she is a patient, humble woman, content to accept her lonely, hard life without complaining. We hear about her early life in rural north Lancashire. Work was very scarce, and her brother, George, who was working in Manchester, found her a place in service there. She came to Manchester as a young girl, and never managed to return, even for a brief visit, to the 'bonny bit' which had been her home. Alice remembers fondly the countryside which she loved, but accepts that 'the pleasure o' helping others' is greater than that of self-indulgence. Whilst she is active, she is always ready to help those in trouble, and is a great comfort to her brother and sister-in-law when their twins die. Her health deteriorates during the course of the book; eventually her mind goes, and she sinks slowly into death, imagining herself back in her childhood life and surroundings. But even as she dies, 'she diffused an atmosphere of peace around her.' (p. 405)

Job Legh, on the other hand, is a more robust character, a knowledgeable, intelligent man, an authority on natural history. It is to him that Mary naturally turns for information and help when she wants to know about alibis, and how to help prove Jem's innocence; it is to him that John turns when he confesses that he is the murderer, and it is to him that Mr Carson turns when he wishes to find out more about John's motives, and to justify his actions as a master. Job conveys a calm, dependable, imperturbable personality, but we also see another side of him in his deep love and concern for his granddaughter, Margaret. There is a delightful interlude in which he describes the journey he and her other grandfather made with the orphaned 'babby' from London, two men with no idea how to feed or comfort the infant, dependent on landladies and chambermaids to help them out. On one occasion the other grandfather puts on a woman's nightcap, with which he hopes to fool the baby but, says Job:

'Such a night as we had on it! Babby began to scream o'th' oud fashion, and we took it turn and turn about to sit up and rock it. My heart were very sore for th' little one, as it groped about wi' its mouth; but for a' that I could scarce keep fra' smiling at th' thought o' us two oud chaps, th' one wi' a woman's night-cap on, sitting on our hinder ends for half th' night, hushabying a babby as wouldn't be hushabied.' (p. 149)

Such gleams of humour indicate Mrs Gaskell's liveliness and sense of the ridiculous, and provide a balance to the prevailing gloom depicted in the lives of the poor.

Jem's mother is another example of a well-drawn, convincing character. Jane Wilson is a 'frabbit' (ill-tempered) woman, who has had much to bear in her life; she had an accident, catching herself against an unboxed wheel in a factory, just before she was married, and this left her sickly and weak. Then, during the course of the story, she loses her twin sons and her husband, and Jem, who becomes the most important person in her life, is on trial for murder. She is indeed shown to have cause for her bitterness and short temper. The overall picture of this unhappy, irritable woman with a deep love for her son, is realistic and adds conviction to the texture of the novel.

There is also a splendid character sketch of Sally Leadbitter, who acts as go-between for Harry Carson and Mary. She is a vulgar, insensitive, self-seeking young woman, incapable of appreciating deep feelings, with 'just talent enough to corrupt others'. (p. 132) Her superficiality is highlighted when she thinks that Mary's only concern at Jem's trial must be over what to wear; she thinks of the trial mainly in terms of picking up young men, and finds it more interesting to continue believing in Jem's guilt: "'Decent men were not going to work with a — no! I suppose I mustn't say it, seeing you went to such trouble to get up an *alibi*.'" (p. 427)

The least real characters, the cardboard cut-outs, are the members of the Carson family. Admittedly they play only a small part in the story, but Mrs Gaskell's lack of sympathy with the masters in this novel is underlined by the lifeless manner in which she characterises them.

Elizabeth Gaskell's love for the countryside in which she grew up is revealed again and again in her writing, and even in a novel such as *Mary Barton*, set almost entirely in the urban environment of an industrial city, it comes bursting through. The book begins and ends in a rural setting: the outing to Green Heys Field at the start, where ' . . . in their seasons may be seen the country business of hay-making, ploughing, &c, which are such pleasant mysteries for townspeople to watch', and where they can ' . . . listen awhile to the delicious sounds of rural life: the lowing of cattle, the milkmaids' call, the clatter and cackle of poultry in the old farmyards'. (p. 39)

At the end, in Canada, Jem and Mary live in:

> . . . a long low wooden house, with room enough, and to spare. The old primeval trees are felled and gone for many a mile around; one alone remains to overshadow the gable-end of the cottage. There is a garden around the dwelling, and far beyond that stretches an orchard. The glory of the Indian summer is over all, making the heart leap at the sight of its gorgeous beauty. (p. 465)

There are also Alice's reminiscences and ramblings about her childhood, in which country life is vividly evoked:

> 'Eh, lasses! ye don't know what rocks are in Manchester! Gray
> pieces o' stone as large as a house, all covered over wi' moss of
> different colours, some yellow, some brown; and the ground
> beneath them knee-deep in purple heather, smelling sae sweet
> and fragrant, and the low music of the humming-bee for ever
> sounding among it.' (p. 70)

The most haunting descriptions are those of the wretched
homes and surroundings of the desperately poor, but the contrast
with the greenness and beauty of nature is powerfully conveyed.

With *Mary Barton* Elizabeth Gaskell achieved recognition and
admiration. It is an authentic account of the effects of poverty and
under-privilege experienced by so many of the inhabitants of the
fast-growing industrial cities, but not recognised or understood
by so many of their affluent and privileged contemporaries. The
authenticity is maintained even in the speech of many of the
characters, and the footnotes which ' . . . form a sort of running
glossary of the Lancashire dialect',[2] were added by her husband,
who had a great interest in, and often lectured on, the local
dialect. She was aware of how her despondency, particularly over
the death of her son, affected her writing, but both the subject-
matter and her own feelings made this inevitable. 'I acknowledge
the fault of there being too heavy a shadow over the book; but I
doubt if the story could have been deeply realised without these
shadows'. (L. 42)

In spite of, or perhaps because of, the shadows, the book made
a great impact when it was first published, and it remains a
powerful account of the lives of *one* of the two nations: the poor.

Notes

1. David Thomson, *England in the Nineteenth Century*, Harmondsworth,
   1950, p. 40.
2. Levitt, 'William Gaskell and the Lancashire Dialect', p. 38.

3 Rural Serenity: *Cranford*

The endearing elegance of female friendship.
Samuel Johnson: *Rasselas*

Cranford, although it is not a novel, is a work of fiction, and although it was based on Knutsford, it exists in its own right as an appropriate home for its various inhabitants. There is no obvious story line, but the episodes are linked by the narrator, by the consistent tone in which it is written, by the underlying principles which govern the life of its community, and by the characters.

Mrs Gaskell considered the first two chapters of *Cranford* (which together formed the first instalment in *Household Words*) as a complete story standing on its own; long afterwards, she explained this to Ruskin: 'The beginning of *Cranford* was *one* paper in *Household Words*; and I never meant to write more, so killed Capt Brown very much against my will'. (L. 562)

The newcomer to *Cranford* finds a small, tightly-knit community: 'It was impossible to live a month at Cranford, and not know the daily habits of each resident'. (p. 49) Through the narrator we get to know the main residents: Miss Jenkyns (Deborah) and her sister, Miss Matilda (known affectionately as Miss Matty, but *not* by her strong-minded sister), who are the pivot of Cranford society. It is Miss Jenkyns who is the arbiter of correct taste and behaviour, but after her death the Honourable Mrs Jamieson takes the lead among the ladies, who include Miss Pole, Mrs Forrester, Mrs Fitz-Adam, Miss Betty Barker and Lady Glenmire. We also meet other characters who spend a limited time in Cranford, including Captain Brown and his two daughters, Signor and Signora Brunoni and poor Peter. The various episodes recounted in the book are more or less self-contained, and the lasting overall impression is of a few well-drawn characters or, in some cases, caricatures, and a number of delightful anecdotes; for example, Captain Brown, who has already disagreed with Miss Jenkyns on the literary merits of Dickens and Johnson, being killed by a train:

When I came to the 'gallant gentleman was deeply engaged in the perusal of a number of *Pickwick*, which he had just received,' Miss Jenkyns shook her head long and solemnly, and then sighed out, 'Poor, dear, infatuated man!' (p. 57)

Another memorable anecdote is the story of Mrs Forrester's lace; she was soaking it in milk to clean it, when her cat drank the milk and swallowed the lace, which was later recovered with the help of currant-jelly and tartar emetic. It survived over many years and was admired by Lady Glenmire, to whom the story is related, with the final explanation:

'I could have kissed her when she returned the lace to sight, very much as it had gone down. Jenny had boiling water ready, and we soaked it and soaked it, and spread it on a lavender-bush in the sun, before I could touch it again, even to put it in milk. But now, your ladyship would never guess that it had been in pussy's inside.' (p. 126)

On a first reading the narrator, Mary Smith, may seem a relatively unimportant, shadowy figure; we do not even find out her name until Chapter 14, and her prime function seems to be to describe the people of Cranford and the texture of its life. However, on considering the tale as a whole, it is evident that she is no mere retailer of events, but on a number of occasions actively participates in and influences those events. She also, by the tone and emphasis of her account, comments on the world she describes and affects the reader's attitude towards it. Mary Smith is an unmarried woman, much younger than most of her Cranford friends. She lives in the big manufacturing town of Drumble (Manchester) some twenty miles away, but makes extended visits to Cranford, usually staying with her close friends, Miss Jenkyns and Miss Matty. Her father, a businessman with a knowledge of financial affairs, makes only one appearance in the story: to help Miss Matty with her financial problems. It is after the death of Miss Jenkyns, who 'had so long taken the lead in Cranford' (p. 64) that Mary Smith begins to take a more active part, especially as Miss Matty needs help and support in arranging her life, for in most things she is 'meek and undecided to a fault.' (p. 67) Mary helps to train Martha, Miss Matty's new servant.

Martha, as instructed, occasionally writes to inform Mary if Miss Matty seems unwell, so our narrator sometimes comes to Cranford unexpectedly in her self-appointed role as Miss Matty's guardian.

The two events in which the narrator initiates the action are both concerned with Miss Matty: first, in the setting up of a business to sell tea and secondly, in the return of Peter, Miss Matty's brother, to Cranford. Miss Matty unfortunately loses almost all her income when the Town and County Bank, in which her money is invested, fails. It is Mary who considers how Miss Matty can supplement her income, who is approached by the ladies of Cranford in their desire to help, and who sees the advantage of Martha marrying her 'follower', Jem Hearn, so that they can set up home with Miss Matty as a lodger. She consults her father about these matters and gets his approval for her ideas, especially for the plan to sell tea, to which Miss Matty agrees with some apprehension. Mary's involvement in this venture continues, and she tells us that: 'I went over from Drumble once a quarter at least, to settle the accounts, and see after the necessary business letters'. (p. 202) The tea-selling business is successful, and after a year we see Miss Matty well established in her new role and, in addition, selling sweets to children. Mary tells us:

I was happy to find that she had made more than twenty pounds during the last year by her sales of tea; and, moreover, that now she was accustomed to it, she did not dislike the employment, which brought her into kindly intercourse with many of the people round about. If she gave them good weight, they, in their turn, brought many a little country present to the 'old rector's daughter'; — a cream cheese, a few new-laid eggs, a little fresh ripe fruit, a bunch of flowers. The counter was quite loaded with these offerings sometimes, as she told me. (p. 205)

Some considerable time before this Miss Matty has told Mary about her brother, Peter, who as a very young man played many practical jokes; his final one had been the impersonation of his elder sister, Deborah, walking with a baby (made from a pillow) in order 'to make something to talk about in the town'. (p. 95) When his father, the rector, found out, he flogged him. Peter ran away to sea and eventually went to India. He had come home once on a visit years later, but had then gone back to India and never been heard of again. Mary hears from Mrs Brown (or Signora Brunoni), who visits Cranford with her conjuror husband, of the family's life in India and the splendid help they received from one Aga Jenkyns. The story fires Mary's imagination: 'Was the "poor Peter" of Cranford the Aga Jenkyns of Chunderabaddad, or was he not? As somebody says, that was the question'. (p. 163) After unsuccessful attempts to find out more facts about Peter, she decides to write direct to 'Aga Jenkyns', to discover if he is 'poor Peter'. For a long time nothing is heard, and Mary tells us:

> I began to be very much ashamed of remembering my letter to the Aga Jenkyns, and very glad I had never named my writing to any one. I only hoped the letter was lost. No answer came. No sign was made. (pp. 202–3)

In the end, however, as a result of Mary's letter, Peter returns; he has not come back before because he thought all the family dead, but now he settles down happily with Miss Matty, bringing enough money to enable her to give up her tea business, to return to her former degree of inconspicuous comfort, and to give handsome presents to all who befriended her during the previous difficult year.

It is clear, then, that the narrator plays a positive role in events in Cranford, initiating and shaping some of the action, but it is through her presentation of events and her comments on them that the reader views the Cranford world with the same tolerant humour as Mary Smith, appreciating the good qualities, but at the same time aware of the eccentric and even ridiculous side of Cranford life. The opening of the book emphasises the belief of the ladies living there of their self-sufficiency — they would not consider it genteel to be referred to as women! We are told that: 'Cranford is in possession of the Amazons' (p. 39) (originally a race of female warriors from Scythia), and their belief that they are inherently superior to men recurs frequently: '"A man," as one of them observed to me once, "is *so* in the way in the house!"' (p. 39) is the generally held view, and Miss Jenkyns 'would have despised the modern idea of women being equal to men. Equal, indeed! she knew they were superior'. (p. 51) Mary Smith is on the whole in sympathy with this feeling: 'My father's was just a man's letter; I mean it was very dull,' she writes (p. 172), and there is a gentle irony in her account of his attitude to one of Miss Jenkyns's investments: '— the only unwise step that clever woman had ever taken, to his knowledge (the only time she ever acted against his advice, I knew).' (p. 172) Sometimes, of course, the Cranford ladies find it convenient to forget their superiority and accept help from a man; so Captain Brown is eventually accepted:

> . . . his excellent masculine common sense, and his facility in devising expedients to overcome domestic dilemmas, had gained him an extraordinary place as authority among the Cranford ladies. (p. 43)

A necessary corollary of the generally prevailing attitude towards men is a suspicion of courtship and matrimony; so Miss Matty and Mary 'felt very uncomfortable and shocked' when Martha tells them she 'likes lads best', (p. 68), and Miss Matty is astounded when she hears of the forthcoming marriage of two Cranford friends, Lady Glenmire and the doctor, Mr Hoggins: '"Marry!" said Miss Matty once again. "Well! I never thought of it. Two people that we know going to be married. It's coming very near!"' (p. 166) Miss Matty, however, is not without sense, and on two occasions at least makes concessions to the man's role in society. In the first instance, she allows Martha to have a follower:

> 'And perhaps, Martha, you may some time meet with a young man you like, and who likes you. I did say you were not to have followers; but if you meet with such a young man, and tell me, and I find he is respectable, I have no objection to his coming to see you once a week.' (p. 82)

This change of attitude occurs when she hears of the death of Thomas Holbrook; long ago there was a love-affair between him and Miss Matty, but it came to nothing, apparently owing to the social snobbery of her father and sister. Miss Matty, it is implied, pines in secret, especially when she hears of his final illness, and then softens her attitude towards Martha: '"God forbid!" said she, in a low voice, "that I should grieve any young hearts."' (p. 82) Her second concession is an admission that men are more practical:

'I don't mean to deny that men are troublesome in a house. I don't judge from my own experience, for my father was neatness itself, and wiped his shoes on coming in as carefully as any woman; but still a man has a sort of knowledge of what should be done in difficulties, that it is very pleasant to have one at hand ready to lean upon.' (p. 180)

At the end of the tale we find Peter happily settled in Cranford, Mr Hoggins and his new wife accepted into Cranford society, and they all attend a luncheon at The George, which restores pleasant, friendly relationships to the whole community, now slightly more balanced with a sprinkling of men, on whom the Amazons are more dependent than they like to admit.

Mary Smith, in her comings and goings between Cranford and Drumble, brings to mind the life of Elizabeth Gaskell herself, especially during the first years of her married life; and the author's awareness of the contrast between life in the busy manufacturing town and that in the peaceful backwater, so far hardly affected by the Industrial Revolution, is made clear. The difference in attitudes engendered by the two environments (and explored much more fully in *North and South*) is evident, and the juxtaposition of these attitudes serves as commentary on them. So, in Cranford, although many of the gentlefolk are poor, 'We none of us spoke of money' (p. 41) and there is great dismay when Captain Brown openly refers to it. All practise 'elegant economy':

'Elegant economy!' How naturally one falls back into the phraseology of Cranford! There, economy was always 'elegant', and money-spending always 'vulgar and ostentatious'; a sort of sour grapeism, which made us very peaceful and satisfied. (p. 42)

Miss Pole succinctly sums up the Cranford viewpoint when she and the other ladies offer secret financial help for Miss Matty:

'I imagine we are none of us what may be called rich, though we all possess a genteel competency, sufficient for tastes that are elegant and refined, and would not, if they could, be vulgarly ostentatious.' (p. 191)

The Drumble outlook is personified in Mary's father, who is 'clear-headed and decisive, and a capital man of business'. (p. 195) On hearing that Miss Matty has salved her conscience about injuring Mr Johnson's business (he also sells tea locally) by discussing her project with him, Mr Smith

> . . . wondered how tradespeople were to get on if there was to be a continual consulting of each other's interest, which would put a stop to all competition directly. (p. 200)

As Mary comments: 'And, perhaps, it would not have done in Drumble, but in Cranford it answered very well'. (p. 200) Even Mr Smith is affected by the simplicity, kindness and generosity which are the hallmarks of Cranford society. When Mary tells him of the offer of financial help by the Cranford ladies:

> He kept brushing his hand before his eyes as I spoke; — and when I went back to Martha's offer the evening before, of receiving Miss Matty as a lodger, he fairly walked away from me to the window, and began drumming with his fingers upon it. Then he turned abruptly round, and said, 'See, Mary, how a good innocent life makes friends all round. Confound it! I could make a good lesson out of it if I were a parson; but as it is, I can't get a tail to my sentences — only I'm sure you feel what I want to say'. (p. 196)

So we are made aware of the virtues of the Cranford outlook, but we are also made aware that big, economic problems have to be solved by the know-how and practicality of the Drumble world. It is Mary Smith, as she moves between the two worlds, who is responsible for many of the practical suggestions, and who helps to implement them, thus emphasising Mrs Gaskell's belief that the energy and drive of the Drumbles must be tempered by the humaneness and sympathy of the Cranfords.

What then are the principles and rules which guide Cranford society? They are summed up neatly by Miss Jenkyns, when she is unable to dissuade Miss Jessie Brown from attending her father's funeral: ' " It is not fit for you to go alone. It would be against both propriety and humanity were I to allow it." ' (p. 57) Propriety and humanity are the two precepts which govern life in Cranford and, to the ladies, they are of equal importance. Mrs Gaskell pokes gentle fun at the propriety and exemplifies the understanding and delicate sensitivity of the humanity.

What was considered appropriate behaviour controls most aspects of Cranford life, so: 'There were rules and regulations for visiting and calls' (p. 40): never visit before twelve, never stay more than a quarter of an hour. 'Genteel' is the word used again and again as a mark of approbation by the Cranford ladies; if behaviour is 'genteel', then it is acceptable. On a visit to Mr Holbrook's, Miss Matty, Miss Pole and Mary have a problem eating their peas, for they are only given two-pronged forks. Miss Matty attempts to spear them with one prong, Miss Pole leaves hers ' . . . for they *would* drop between the prongs', but our narrator tells us:

> I looked at my host: the peas were going wholesale into his capacious mouth, shovelled up by his large round-ended knife. I saw, I imitated, I survived! My friends, in spite of my precedent, could not muster up courage enough to do an ungenteel thing. (p. 75)

The ladies of Cranford mistrust the modern world of trade and industry which dominates Drumble, considering those involved in it socially inferior, and Mrs Gaskell mildly satirises their attitude towards it. Miss Betty Barker is slightly hesitant about extending an invitation to Mary Smith because of her connection with Drumble:

> She gave me also an impromptu invitation, as I happened to be a visitor; though I could see she had a little fear lest, since my father had gone to live in Drumble, he might have engaged in that 'horrid cotton trade', and so dragged his family down out of 'aristocratic society'. (p. 106)

As Mary comments, Miss Barker 'was no democrat and understood the difference of ranks.' (p. 107) None of Cranford society 'spoke of money, because that subject savoured of commerce and trade, and though some might be poor, we were all aristocratic' (p. 41), and Miss Jessie Brown's admission that she had an uncle who was a shopkeeper shocks the assembled ladies, who do their best to keep the information from the Honourable Mrs Jamieson, for ' . . .what would she say or think, if she found out she was in the same room with a shopkeeper's niece!' (p. 46)

So the various Cranford proprieties are satirised, and Mary's comments place them in a slightly ridiculous light, but it is always done with a light, refreshing touch. The humanity, on the other hand, is presented with understanding and admiration. We have already seen how the ladies respond to Miss Matty's misfortune, and we are told that:

> . . . for kindness (somewhat dictatorial) to the poor, and real tender good offices to each other whenever they are in distress, the ladies of Cranford are quite sufficient. (p. 39)

There is another memorable example, when Miss Matty herself shows a sense of responsibility and caring towards a Mr Dobson; he has presented a note from the Town and County Bank, which the shop does not accept because of rumours that the bank has failed. Miss Matty insists on exchanging his now worthless note for five sovereigns: '"Why! then it will only have been common honesty in me, as a shareholder, to have given this good man the money."' (p. 177) Her 'common honesty' leaves Miss Matty with about five shillings a week to live on, but far from regretting having given her five sovereigns away, she explains that: '" I was very thankful, that I saw my duty this morning, with the poor man standing by me."' (p. 179)

The ladies of Cranford, although sharing the same basic attitudes, are all individuals and, over the course of the book, we build up a picture of each one. Miss Pole, rather outspoken, is a militant spinster; she sees herself as clear-headed, not fooled by Signor Brunoni's conjuring tricks, nor by tales of ghosts, nor by apparent male imperturbability. She sums men up, saying:

> 'If you will notice, they have always foreseen events, though they never tell one for one's warning before the events happen; my father was a man, and I know the sex pretty well.' (p. 145)

She affects great bravery when there are rumours of robberies in the neighbourhood, but is in fact as fearful as everyone else, rushing to spend the night at Miss Matty's when she imagines she will be the victim. She is the first to find out about local happenings, and loves to astonish her audience. When she feels slighted by Mrs Jamieson, she is highly indignant and sarcastic, but is quite ready to overlook the offence as soon as she has the opportunity of meeting Lady Glenmire and showing off her smart new cap. At heart, though, she is full of the humanity and kindness which are so important in Cranford, and it is she who organises the offers of help for Miss Matty.

Mrs Forrester is a gentle, kindly widow, very concerned about propriety; she is openly nervous and not ashamed to admit her fear of ghosts. She has very little to live on, but is as ready to help Miss Matty as any of the other ladies, even though her contribution 'will necessitate many careful economies, and many pieces of self-denial.' (p. 193)

The Honourable Mrs Jamieson is a comparatively wealthy, self-indulgent widow. She is manipulated by her superior man-servant, Mr Mulliner, and:

> . . . if she had two characteristics in her natural state of health, they were a facility for eating and sleeping. If she could neither eat nor sleep, she must be indeed out of spirits and out of health. (p. 144)

Mrs Jamieson prefers to mix with County families, and is insensitive to the feelings of the Cranford ladies; her snobbery results in her ignoring Mrs Fitz-Adam's existence and refusing to acknowledge her sister-in-law, Lady Glenmire, after the latter's marriage to Mr Hoggins. She is, however, susceptible to flattery, and is eventually won round by Peter, who arranges an entertainment at The George 'Under the Patronage of the HONOURABLE MRS JAMIESON'. (p. 216) She is also, Peter finds, very gullible, and he hoodwinks her with many fantastic stories but, as he explains to Mary: '"I consider Mrs Jamieson fair game."' (p. 217)

Miss Jenkyns (as Miss Matty frequently informs us) was very clever and considered herself literary. She effortlessly took control in a crisis and was never floored. When she died, 'something of the clear knowledge of the strict code of gentility went out too'.

(p. 109) Miss Barker, the daughter of the former clerk at Cranford, had previously run a milliner's shop with her sister. After such beginnings, she is infinitely grateful to be accepted in Cranford society, and even considers it a compliment that Mrs Jamieson should feel so much at home in her house as to fall asleep! It was she who dressed her cow, 'a mark of respectability in Cranford' (p. 106) in a grey flannel waistcoat (on the suggestion of Captain Brown) after it had fallen into a lime-pit. Mrs Fitz-Adam, the widowed sister of Mr Hoggins, is well-to-do; she is a self-effacing, pleasant woman, very conscious of the fact that she had been ' . . . nothing but a country girl, coming to market with eggs and butter, and such like things'. (p. 194) She is not offended by Mrs Jamieson's overlooking her, but always makes her a deep curtsey, and is delighted and astonished at having 'a ladyship' as a sister-in-law. She is sensitive to the feelings of others and therefore aware of the difficulty of giving Miss Matty as much as she can afford: 'She told me she thought she never could look Miss Matty in the face again if she presumed to be giving her so much as she should like to do.' (p. 194)

However, the character who is most fully drawn, and who occupies a central place in many of the events, is Miss Matty. She is a quiet, timid person, reluctant to give an opinion of her own, who has obviously been dominated by her father and elder sister. As a result, many of her feelings and wishes have been repressed, and she has led a sad, unfulfilled life. She admires her elder sister enormously, and constantly refers to her, always emphasising Deborah's superiority, cleverness, knowledge of correct forms, and general good sense. In contrast, her opinion of her own qualities is very low: '"I knew I was good for little, and that my best work in the world was to do odd jobs quietly, and set others at liberty.' (p. 103) She is excessively nervous, and admits to rolling a ball under the bed at night to discover whether anyone is hiding there; she also institutes elaborate precautions to protect the house during the robbery scare.

Her love affair with Mr Holbrook came to an end because of the attitude of her father and sister, and she is left with a fear of men and a deep suspicion of courting and matrimony. When she is about to set up her tea business, she finds some comfort in the thought that men do not buy tea: ' . . . and it was of men particularly she was afraid. They had such sharp loud ways with them; and did up accounts, and counted their change so quickly!' (p. 198) When she discovers a gentleman in the drawing-room with his arm round Miss Jessie Brown's waist: 'Miss Matty's eyes looked large with terror', (p. 61) '. . .her eyes were round with affright' (p. 104) on hearing a strange noise like kissing. She is extremely naïve about anything relating to sex, and does not even realise that Martha is about to have a baby until Mary tells her; she is, however, delighted when the baby arrives, and ' . . . looked at it curiously with a sort of tender wonder at its small perfection of parts.' (p. 204) The repression which she has suffered, and which has turned her into an insecure, nervous, anxious woman, is sadly reflected when she says: '"I only hope it is not improper; so many pleasant things are!"' (p. 75)

We do, however, see another side to Miss Matty's character: the self-control and quiet dignity with which she behaves when she is sure of herself. These are evident in her reception of Mrs Jamieson, when that lady makes it clear that she does not wish the Cranford ladies to call on Lady Glenmire, and also in the episode of Mr Dobson and the five sovereigns.

To sum up the character and influence of Miss Matty and the atmosphere of Cranford itself, one cannot do better than turn to the final paragraph:

Ever since that day there has been the old friendly sociability in Cranford society; which I am thankful for, because of my dear Miss Matty's love of peace and kindliness. We all love Miss Matty, and I somehow think we are all of us better when she is near us. (p. 218)

It was a book which gave lasting pleasure to its author; as she wrote to Ruskin shortly before her death, it was the only one of her books she could re-read and laugh over, remembering especially the cow in its grey flannel jacket, which she had actually seen, and the cat that swallowed the lace, which she had known.

4 The Fallen Woman: *Ruth*

A boy like that wants one thing only
And when he's done, he'll leave you lonely.
Stephen Sondheim: *West Side Story*

The most startling departure from existing literary convention made by Mrs Gaskell in *Ruth* was not that she wrote about the Fallen Woman, but that she made her the central character. For example, Lydia Bennet in *Pride and Prejudice*, Esther in *Mary Barton* and Little Em'ly in *David Copperfield* are all victims of unscrupulous, self-seeking men, as is Ruth, but none of them is of major importance in the story, and all are 'swept under the carpet' in a manner that was acceptable to nineteenth-century moral principles: Lydia is made 'honest' by marrying her seducer; Esther dies after a life of prostitution; and Em'ly is shipped off to Australia. Death or emigration was indeed the favourite Victorian recipe for dealing with this unpalatable social problem, but Mrs Gaskell, as the wife of a Unitarian minister, was too closely involved with such situations to feel that the fate she outlined for Esther, prostitution and deprivation leading to sickness and death, was the best that could be hoped for. Elizabeth Gaskell was so concerned about one girl in particular that she enlisted the help of Dickens and of her friend, Eliza Fox, during 1849 and 1850 and succeeded in sending this girl to the Cape, thus giving her a new start in life. She was, however, determined to show that it was possible for a young woman to turn her back on an unfortunate episode, and to become, even after such a beginning, a useful and respected member of society; so she depicts Ruth, deserted by her lover, slowly and painstakingly proving her worth to those amongst whom she lives.

Mrs Gaskell, however, was not content with tackling only this thorny social problem, but also introduced into the story the result of Ruth's seduction, the illegitimate child, and portrayed the problems facing him. Ruth's attempt to provide a secure and loving environment for her son, Leonard, was yet another challenge to Victorian attitudes. Elizabeth Gaskell is also concerned with the harmful consequences of basing conduct on a lie, however well-intentioned the motives. Her belief in the necessity for truthfulness, whatever unpleasantness might result, is a recurring theme in her work. She stresses its importance elsewhere, in *North and South* and in *Sylvia's Lovers*, for example.

Ruth Hilton, left an orphan at an early age, is apprenticed to a dressmaker, Mrs Mason, who exploits her young work-women, showing little interest in them apart from their work. Ruth suffers from loneliness and lack of friendship in the town where she must now live, and is therefore susceptible to the kindness shown her by Mr Bellingham, a selfish, spoilt young man with whom she is thrown into contact. Mrs Mason by chance comes upon Ruth and Mr Bellingham during one of their outings, and immediately dismisses Ruth, thus leaving her without lodgings as well as without employment. Not yet sixteen, 'obedient and docile by nature, and unsuspicious and innocent of any harmful consequences' (p. 60) she easily succumbs to Mr Bellingham's suggestion that she should accompany him to London. We next see Ruth and her lover living at an inn in North Wales, an area which Mrs Gaskell loved, and which she describes vividly. When Mr Bellingham falls very ill, the innkeeper sends for his mother, who takes control, removing her son as soon as it is possible, and dismissing Ruth with a £50 note and the advice that she should enter a penitentiary, an institution for the reformation of character. Ruth, quite desolate, is saved from suicide by Thurstan Benson, a hunchbacked Dissenting minister, on holiday in the same Welsh village as Ruth. He and his sister, Faith, take Ruth, now found to be pregnant, to their home in Eccleston (based on Newcastle), and introduce her as Mrs Denbigh, a distant relation, supposedly recently widowed. Ruth settles down with the Bensons and their strong-charactered elderly servant, Sally, who is almost a part of the family. Ruth's son, Leonard, is born, and for some time all is peaceful, although Ruth's presence adds to the financial problems of the Bensons, a fact of which she is well aware, and which she wishes to alleviate. Eventually the opportunity comes, when she is offered the post of governess to Mr Bradshaw's daughters. He is Mr Benson's most influential congregant, a self-righteous, outspoken man, very conscious of his position in the world, and not prepared to show any sympathy towards those he considers guilty of weakness or wrong-doing.

During her period as governess, a position which she fills with love and conscientiousness, Ruth meets the local parliamentary candidate, who is a protégé of Mr Bradshaw. He turns out to be Ruth's seducer, Mr Bellingham, who is now known as Mr Donne. He is again captivated by her, and tries to persuade her to become his mistress once more. On her refusal (and reminiscent of Harry Carson in *Mary Barton*), he offers to marry her, but she rejects this also, saying she no longer loves him. She fears he will try to take Leonard from her, but eventually he leaves her in peace.

The secret of Ruth's and Leonard's background does, however, leak out. It results in instant dismissal for her by Mr Bradshaw, and in disgrace for Faith and Thurstan Benson for having concealed Ruth's origins and thus imposed on Mr Bradshaw. A time of great difficulty for the Bensons, Ruth and Leonard ensues, but Ruth finally finds employment as a sicknurse, an occupation for which she has particular gifts of sympathy, tenderness and concern, and she thus becomes much respected and sought after professionally in Eccleston. The climax of this career comes when a typhus epidemic reaches the town, and Ruth's bravery and nursing skill win her great acclaim. Hearing that Mr Donne is lying ill in a local hotel, she insists on nursing him. In the end he recovers, but Ruth catches the fever and dies. Mr Donne, until now unknown to Thurstan Benson as Leonard's father, offers money for the boy's education, but this is indignantly refused. ' "Leonard is not unprovided for. Those that honoured his mother will take care of him." ' (p. 450) Many people come to Mr Benson's church (based on the Unitarian chapel in Knutsford) to hear his funeral sermon, so testifying to the fact that Ruth has established herself as a worthy woman in their eyes; amongst them comes Mr Bradshaw 'to testify his respect for the woman, who, if all had entertained his opinions, would have been driven into hopeless sin.' (p. 453)

Ruth's innocence is repeatedly emphasised: for example, she 'was innocent and snow-pure' (p. 43): 'Remember how young, and innocent, and motherless she was!' (p. 56); 'She's an innocent, inoffensive young creature' (p. 77). She was therefore slow to realise the view society would take of her behaviour, and was deeply shocked when she first became aware of this: 'She could not put into words the sense she was just beginning to entertain of the estimation in which she was henceforward to be held'. (p. 72) The reasons why Ruth succumbs to temptation are well illustrated in the depressing picture Mrs Gaskell paints of her life at Mrs Mason's. It is clear that she will grasp at any opportunity of friendship, and when she loses her place at Mrs Mason's will find it difficult to re-establish herself on her own, being young, immature, weak, lonely and without the support of a responsible adult. It does, however, stretch the reader's credulity to accept that, even though she is barely sixteen, she is so unaware of how her actions will be viewed by the society in which she lives. There are, in fact, indications that she is worried about the morality of her behaviour even before she goes to London and then to Wales with her lover:

'How strange it is,' she thought that evening, 'that I should feel as if this charming afternoon's walk were, somehow, not exactly wrong, but yet as if it were not right.' (p. 40)

Is she really so ignorant, and therefore innocent, as Elizabeth Gaskell seems to insist? Is she really so taken by surprise when she is treated with contempt at the inn in Wales? It was, of course, important from Mrs Gaskell's point of view, if she was finally to establish Ruth as a woman of worth, to insist that there was nothing inherently depraved in her character; that she was inveigled into wrong-doing by lack of knowledge and not through disregard of the moral laws she was breaking. With the exception of this initial lapse from Victorian moral standards, Ruth is portrayed as a young woman who is the embodiment of virtuous behaviour and right-thinking attitudes. She nurses Mr Bellingham with tireless devotion until his mother arrives: 'Exceeding love supplied the place of experience' (p. 79) and even Mr Bellingham tells his mother that 'Ruth is no improper character' and ' . . . I led her wrong'. (p. 88) She accepts with humility and gentleness the plan proposed by the Bensons, because she is determined to do the best for her unborn child. Faith Benson, at first ready to judge her harshly, explains to her brother: 'It is almost impossible to help being kind to her; there is something so meek and gentle about her, so patient, and so grateful!' (p. 123), whilst Sally, who decides to cut off Ruth's beautiful curls 'in a merciless manner', considering them a disgrace for a 'widow', is touched with compunction by the 'sad gentleness' with which Ruth submits. Mr Bradshaw approves of 'her quiet manner' and considers her a respectable young person:

> . . . lovely, quiet Ruth, with her low tones and soft replies, her delicate waving movements, appeared to him the very type of what a woman should be — a calm, serene soul, fashioning the body to angelic grace. (p. 305)

But Ruth is not a static character; she develops into a selfless, devoted mother, she learns to control her sorrow and to tackle whatever she does with 'a vigour and cheerfulness', particularly after Sally lectures her on:

> ' . . . a right and a wrong way of setting about everything — and to my thinking, the right way is to take a thing up heartily, if it is only making a bed.' (p. 173)

Perhaps the most striking evidence of Ruth's growth in stature is seen in the interview she has with Mr Donne, as Mr Bellingham is now known, when they meet at Mr Bradshaw's holiday home at Abermouth. When she first realises his identity, she is deeply confused, and thinks of him with affection. ' "Oh, darling love! am I talking against you?" asked she tenderly. "I am so torn and perplexed! You, who are the father of my child!" ' (p. 270). Slowly, however, and through prayer, she begins to see more clearly: 'Oh, my God! I do believe Leonard's father is a bad man' (p. 271), and when she observes him closely, she realises that he has changed: ' . . . the expression, which had been only occasional formerly, when his worse self predominated, had become permanent. He looked restless and dissatisfied.' (p. 275)

When he finds out who she is, and also about Leonard's existence, he demands an interview with her. She is strong enough and clear-sighted enough to acknowledge the truth, that she loved him and was happy with him formerly, but she tells him forthrightly that it would be a far greater sin for her to go back to him now: ' "What I did wrong then, I did blindly to what I should do now if I listened to you." ' (p. 296) Her strength and maturity, her growth from an ignorant, rather weak and easily flattered girl, are convincingly demonstrated when she refuses the offer of marriage which he makes as the only way (so he thinks) of securing her:

> 'I do not love you. I did once. Don't say I did not love you then! but I do not now. I could never love you again. All you have said and done since you came with Mr Bradshaw to Abermouth first has only made me wonder how I ever could have loved you. We are very far apart. The time that has pressed down my life like brands of hot iron, and scarred me for ever, has been nothing to you.' (pp. 299–300)

When she finally sees him for what he is, she refuses, with feeling and dignity, to let him come into contact with Leonard:

> 'You shall have nothing to do with my boy, by my consent, much less by my agency. I would rather see him working on the roadside than leading such a life — being such a one as you are.' (p. 300)

Ruth's honesty and courage are again evident when she decides that it must be she who tells Leonard the truth about his birth. She makes clear to him that what *she* did was wrong, and that they will *both* suffer for it, but she assures him that ' " . . . it is only your own sin that can make you an outcast from God," ' (p. 342) and that *he* has committed no sin. As the story draws to an end, a picture of Ruth as a woman of understanding and sympathy, of self-command and humility is drawn. Elizabeth Gaskell, by making Ruth develop into such a woman, showed, as she had intended, that a fallen woman is not beyond redemption; the extremely adverse response of the public to the novel took her by surprise: 'I think I must be an improper woman without knowing it', she wrote, 'I do so manage to shock people.' (L. 150)

Leonard's problems as an illegitimate child, although not as central to the novel as those of Ruth, form a different aspect of this social problem. Leonard himself is a wooden character, not convincing, but the difficulties occasioned by his illegitimacy are clearly dealt with. Faith Benson's immediate reaction on hearing that Ruth is pregnant is to refer to the baby as: 'This disgrace — this badge of her shame' (p. 118) and as: 'this miserable offspring of sin' (p. 119), but both her brother and Ruth, independently of each other, always emphasise the innocence of the child. Faith, in fact, is soon won round to her brother's way of thinking. Leonard grows to the age of twelve in a happy, secure environment, unaware of the truth until Ruth has to tell him. As a result he changes from a contented, trusting child into a suspicious, frightened boy, unwilling even to go into the street: '. . . dreading to be pointed at as an object of remark'. (p. 362) At first, his attitude to his mother changes, and he becomes sullen and resentful, but gradually he responds to Ruth's love and example and, with her at least, he re-establishes a more normal relationship. Finally, he accepts Ruth's worth when he hears her praised for her services to the sick by a crowd of poor people in the street, and then proudly acknowledges his relationship to her: ' "Sir, I am her son!" ' (p. 426) He is immediately respected and blessed by the crowd, and: 'From that day forward Leonard walked erect in the streets of Eccleston, where 'many arose and called her blessed." ' (p. 426)

Mrs Gaskell did not flinch from her insistence that, however blameworthy the parents might be, an illegitimate child bore no blame or guilt; it was an unpopular attitude to hold in the 1850s, so different from the more common response attributed to Mr Bradshaw: ' "Do you suppose that he is ever to rank with other boys, who are not stained and marked with sin from their birth?" ' (pp. 336–7) But even Mr Bradshaw, the apparent upholder of Victorian attitudes of moral rectitude, implicitly admits that he has judged Ruth wrongly, when he attends the service in her memory at Thurstan Benson's church and, in an unnecessarily sentimental ending, shows that his attitude towards her son has been equally unjust. He meets Leonard by Ruth's grave, and is so moved by the boy's grief that he speaks to him with great kindness, and is overcome by 'the sympathy which choked up his voice, and filled his eyes with tears.' (p. 454)

Nor did Mrs Gaskell flinch from considering the dilemma facing the Bensons when they decide to look after Ruth: how to persuade the hostile society of their time to give a chance to the unmarried mother and illegitimate child. The Bensons, with Faith as the instigator of the plan, the 'temptress', as it were, take the easier way out: they hide the truth, rather than face the condemnation and cruelty which would otherwise have resulted, and which Ruth and her child would also have had to face: 'It was the decision — the pivot, on which the fate of years moved.' (p. 121) It is a decision which causes Thurstan Benson continual worry: ' "You don't know how this apparent necessity for falsehood pains me, Faith" ', he tells his sister, who has just invented many more details of Ruth's early life, and has admitted: ' "I am afraid I enjoy not being fettered by truth".' (p. 149) When he is finally confronted by Mr Bradshaw with his lie, Thurstan admits that for years he has suffered from his deceit, but attempts to justify himself by explaining: ' "You, sir, know how terribly the world goes against all such as have sinned as Ruth did." ' (p. 345) He goes on to make an impassioned plea for all fallen women to be given a chance of self-redemption, but he condemns his own weakness in yielding to temptation and not facing up to the truth. In this scene Thurstan Benson is clearly expressing Mrs Gaskell's own conviction that the unmarried mother should be given the opportunity to rehabilitate herself, but that deceit, although occasioned by selfless, even praiseworthy motives, is unacceptable and indeed 'wrong and faithless'. We see Elizabeth Gaskell courageously incorporating her own deeply held views and high moral standards into her writing.

The hypocrisy of many of the 'pillars of society' is neatly satirised in the characterisation of Mr Bradshaw. His outraged indignation against those failing to conform to society's accepted rules of conduct is directed not only against Ruth and the Bensons, but even against his own son, whom he disowns on discovering that he has been guilty of forgery. However, in his determination to ensure that *his* protégé is elected to parliament, Mr Bradshaw tacitly sanctions bribery:

> He hoped that Mr Pilson [the agent] did not mean to allude to bribery; but he did not express this hope, because he thought it would deter the agent from using this means, and it was possible it might prove to be the only way. (p. 248)

Elizabeth Gaskell was indeed well aware of the double standards of which men of Mr Bradshaw's openly flaunted views might be guilty.

Her skill in character-drawing is especially evident in her presentation of minor characters, and this is well exemplified in her portrayal of Sally, the Bensons' servant. She is a warm, lively person, on familiar, easy terms with her employers, whom she has known since they were young children, and who consider her as part of the family. She is a somewhat formidable character, of whom even Faith is occasionally afraid; indeed she does not dare to tell Sally the truth about Ruth, but leaves it to her brother; it proves to be a less terrible task than Faith fears, for Ruth's sweet submissiveness has already tempered Sally's abrasiveness. Sally's impulsive love and sympathy are demonstrated when she interferes to prevent Thurstan from whipping Leonard for untruthfulness. There is also a delicate irony when she says:

> 'I think it's for them without sin to throw stones at a poor child and cut up good laburnum-branches to whip him. I only do as my betters do, when I call Leonard's mother Mrs Denbigh.' (p. 202)

One delightful episode concerning Sally is her description of her sweethearts. It is full of a kindly humour, and we laugh with, not at, Sally in her naïveté and ingenuousness. Her offers of marriage come firstly from John Rawson, a madman who, she decides later, on despairing of ever receiving another offer, was not so very mad, but '" . . . it were only his way to go about on all-fours, but that he was a sensible man in most things" ' (p. 164), and secondly from Jerry Dixon, who tells her:

> ' "I'll wait till Christmas," says he. "I've a pig as will be ready for killing then, so I must get married before that." Well now! would you believe it? the pig was a temptation. I'd a receipt for curing hams, as Miss Faith would never let me try, saying the old way were good enough. However, I resisted.' (p. 167)

The use of delicate humour is reminiscent of *Cranford*.

Many of the other characters in *Ruth* are memorable: Thurstan Benson, physically deformed, but with 'a mild beauty of the face', racked by doubts at the deception he is practising, yet proving himself a thoroughly good and sensitive man; Mr Bellingham shallow and self-indulgent; Mrs Bradshaw pliant, dominated by her husband, yet eventually showing the depth of her maternal love, and her daughter, Jemima, passionate, impatient

49

and outspoken, who matures from a rather flighty girl into a dependable woman.

There are fine descriptions, both of indoor scenes (for example the shire-hall to which Ruth goes as a young milliner, and Sally's kitchen) and the countryside to which Elizabeth Gaskell always responded so freshly and sensitively; this is especially evident in her descriptions of the Welsh landscape. The impact of colour and light in her descriptions seems particularly characteristic of *Ruth*. For example, in North Wales:

> . . . she saw the swift-fleeting showers come athwart the sunlight like a rush of silver arrows; she watched the purple darkness on the heathery mountain-side, and then the pale golden gleam which succeeded. (p. 64)

or in the Bensons' garden:

> The long jessamine sprays, with their white-scented stars, forced themselves almost into the room. The little square garden beyond, with grey stone walls all round, was rich and mellow in its autumnal colouring, running from deep crimson hollyhocks up to amber and gold nasturtiums, and all toned down by the clear and delicate air. (p. 139)

Colour is even used metaphorically to express a mood; so, when the Benson household is struggling after Ruth's secret becomes known:

> . . . their peace was as the stillness of a grey autumnal day, when no sun is to be seen above, and when a quiet film seems drawn before both sky and earth, as if to rest the wearied eyes after the summer's glare. (p. 373)

It is important to realise that there was no element of permissiveness in Elizabeth Gaskell's championship of Ruth. Her attitude is well expressed by Mr Benson, when he tries to make Mr Bradshaw understand that ' . . . not every woman who has fallen is depraved', but that ' . . . many crave and hunger after a chance of virtue'. (p. 347) What would Ruth's future have been if the Bensons had not protected and supported her, and was she not worthy of that protection and support? These are the questions posed by the story. But Mrs Gaskell was no rebel against the prevailing condemnation of immoral behaviour. When she discovered that the author of *Adam Bede*, a book she greatly admired, was Mary Ann Evans (George Eliot's real name), and that Miss Evans was living with a married man, she found this difficult to accept:

> It is a noble grand book, whoever wrote it, — but Miss Evans' life taken at the best construction, does so jar against the beautiful book that one cannot help hoping against hope. (L. 438)

She also tacitly accepted the Victorian double standard for men's and women's behaviour: what was folly or carelessness in a man, a passing episode, was a lifetime's tragedy for a woman, something which she could only overcome, if at all, by a totally pure and virtuous life afterwards. As Richard Bradshaw says (although in a different context): ' "Oh! many things are right for men which are not for girls." ' (p. 211) Elizabeth Gaskell regarded the fallen woman with humanity, sympathy and understanding, but she never condoned her behaviour.

5 The Industrial Scene — Second Thoughts: *North and South*

> All reform except a moral one will prove unavailing.
> Carlyle: *Corn Law Rhymes*

By the time Mrs Gaskell came to write *North and South* she had achieved a considerable literary reputation. Dickens had written: 'I do honestly know that there is no living English writer whose aid I would desire to enlist in preference to the authoress of *Mary Barton*'.[1] He had already published *Cranford* and several of her short stories in *Household Words*. He was now prepared to accept a full-length novel, and *North and South* appeared in twenty-two weekly instalments, starting in September 1854.

This method of publication was becoming very popular, and resulted in new novels reaching a much wider public than previously. It did, however, have drawbacks, and although Mrs Gaskell continued to write for periodicals (for *Household Words* and *All the Year Round* for Dickens, published weekly, and later for the *Cornhill* for Smith, Elder, published monthly), she found the limitations imposed by this method troublesome and difficult. She did not find it easy to meet the frequently recurring deadlines, and this led to friction with the publishers, but, more importantly, her conception of her novels as a unity, in which the main characters develop gradually to maturity and self-realisation, did not lend itself readily to division into instalments. To meet the demands of serial publication not only do the units have to be of fairly even length, but also either episodic and more or less self-contained, or else rise on each occasion to a climax which will keep the reader waiting in suspense for the next issue. *Cranford* fitted into the first category, so that each instalment was in many ways complete in itself, although obviously more interesting and enjoyable taken as part of the whole, but Mrs Gaskell's full-length novels did not fit comfortably into either category. This led to problems between her and Dickens about suitable points at which to end instalments, and made it very difficult for her to

than appears at this stage. The very vagueness with which Mr
Hale explains the doubts which cause him to leave the Church is
probably a clue to the minor importance of the religious theme.
However, in one form or another, it does recur throughout
the novel. Mr Hale's display of integrity in resigning from his
comfortable living is presented in a favourable light. There is a
conflict about religion between Bessy, a devout Christian, and
her agnostic father, Nicholas; as he tells Margaret:

> 'I say, leave a' this talk about religion alone, and set to work on
> what yo' see and know. That's my creed. It's simple, and not
> far to fetch, nor hard to work.' (p. 133)

But when, after Bessy's death, Higgins visits Margaret's father,
his attitude has mellowed, so that: 'Margaret the Churchwoman,
her father the Dissenter, Higgins the Infidel, knelt down together.
It did them no harm'. (p. 297)

The main theme of the story, the conflict between the attitudes
of Mr Thornton and Margaret, between North and South, and
their eventual understanding and appreciation of each other,
does not begin to emerge until Chapter 7, when Margaret arrives
in Milton Northern and first meets Mr Thornton. Taking the
novel as a whole, this start 'in such an oblique fashion' (p. 8) is
justified, but it was hardly suited to the serial method of publication! However, before Margaret meets Mr Thornton, we have
been prepared for their conflict by her attitude to trade and
commerce: '"I don't like shoppy people,"' she says (p. 50) and,
on hearing of her father's plans for private tutoring in the North,
she exclaims: '"What in the world do manufacturers want with
the classics, or literature, or the accomplishments of a gentleman?"' (p. 72)

The prejudice and the pride with which the two main characters respond to each other has been mentioned briefly by one or
two critics as reminiscent of Jane Austen's novel *Pride and Prejudice*, published in 1813. There are, in fact, many parallels: Mr
Hale refers to Thornton as ' . . . a man who is far too proud to
show his feelings.' (p. 221) and almost immediately tells Margaret
that she is ' . . . quite prejudiced against Mr Thornton.' (p. 221)
When Thornton first proposes, he is dismissed with scorn by
Margaret, as is Darcy by Elizabeth, and both heroes later pro-

pose a second time. After the first proposal, Margaret's attitude begins to soften in a way reminiscent of Elizabeth's change of feeling towards Darcy:

> When he was gone, she thought she had seen the gleam of unshed tears in his eyes; and that turned her proud dislike into something different and kinder, if nearly as painful — self-reproach for having caused such mortification to anyone. (p. 255)

A discussion between Margaret and Mr Thornton on what is comprised by the terms 'gentleman' and 'true man' (pp. 217–18) brings to mind the discussion between Elizabeth Bennet and Darcy on what they comprehend by the term 'accomplished woman'. Margaret, after receiving near the beginning of the novel a proposal from Henry Lennox: ' . . . made a strong effort to be calm; she would not speak till she had succeeded in mastering her voice' (p. 61), whilst we are told that Darcy, on being rejected by Elizabeth, ' . . . was struggling for the appearance of composure, and would not open his lips, till he believed himself to have attained it'.[3]

When Thornton's mother suggests to Margaret that she is behaving improperly in walking with a gentleman far from home in the evening, Margaret's disdainful reply is similar to Elizabeth's rejection of Lady Catherine de Bourgh's interference in her affairs. Margaret says: '"You can say nothing more, Mrs Thornton. I decline every attempt to justify myself for anything. You must allow me to leave the room"' (p. 394) whilst Elizabeth tells Lady Catherine: '"You can *now* have nothing further to say. . . . You have insulted me, in every possible method. I must beg to return to the house".'[4] The similarities are perhaps coincidental, but serve to emphasise Mrs Gaskell's primary concern with the developing relationship and understanding between a man and woman who are at first totally opposed to each other, a concern similar to that of Jane Austen in *Pride and Prejudice*.

When they first meet, Margaret and Thornton are separated as much by their attitudes towards others as by their response to the industry and power of Milton Northern. For Margaret, the human interest is all-important. She becomes gradually reconciled to life in Milton after meeting Bessy and Nicholas Higgins:

from the very fact that it is not engaged in trade. She gradually comes to respect many of the inhabitants of Milton and, in her turn, is surprised at Frederick's reaction to Thornton as ' . . . someone of a different class, not a gentleman', and is then ashamed as she remembers how, at first, 'before she knew his character, she had spoken and thought of him just as Frederick was doing'. (p. 324) But, in spite of her greater understanding and tolerance in this respect, she never wavers from her belief that humanity and not commerce should regulate human relationships, and Thornton in his turn becomes more understanding and tolerant, so that the gap narrows between Margaret's attitude and his own. He explains that his 'only wish is to have the opportunity of cultivating some intercourse with the hands beyond mere "cash nexus".' (p. 525)

Margaret is indirectly responsible for Thornton's employing Higgins after the strike, and for the subsequent acquaintance of the two men on a more personal level. This leads to a much greater awareness by them both of the problems of the other side of industry, and to some interesting changes in their outlooks. The most significant of these is Thornton's increasing interest in the general welfare of his men. He takes upon himself some of the responsibility of providing for the Boucher children, now orphaned, and, even more significantly, he builds a dining-room for his employees for, as he explains: ' . . . by buying things wholesale, and cooking a good quantity of provisions together, much money might be saved, and much comfort gained'. (p. 445) This plan is at first rejected by Higgins, and Thornton therefore 'laid it aside, both as impracticable, and also because if I forced it into operation I should be interfering with the independence of my men'. (p. 445) This marks an interesting symbiosis of Margaret's and Thornton's ideas: he is now prepared to consider the more general welfare of his workmen (whom he now refers to as 'men' rather than 'hands'), but he still respects their independence and will not force his scheme upon them. He then explains in a good-humoured manner how the plan was eventually launched:

' . . . suddenly, this Higgins came to me and graciously signified his approval of a scheme so nearly the same as mine, that I might fairly have claimed it; . . . But it seemed childish to relinquish a plan which I had once thought wise and well laid, just because I myself did not receive all the honour and consequence due to the originator'. (p. 445)

What a change there has been in Thornton's attitude, and how much nearer is his approach to that of Margaret! But when Mr Bell, to whom he has explained the scheme, offers a £10 note, to 'give the poor fellows a feast' (p. 446), Thornton tells him:

'I don't want it to fall into a charity. I don't want donations. Once let in the principle, and I should have people going and talking, and spoiling the simplicity of the whole thing.' (p. 446)

This plan represents the kind of mutual help and interdependence which Elizabeth Gaskell would have welcomed as a solution to industrial problems, rather than the conflict of a strike. In both *Mary Barton* and *North and South* she represents a strike as harmful to both sides, causing great hardship and much ill-feeling: 'So class distrusted class, and their want of mutual confidence wrought sorrow to both'.[6] In *Mary Barton*, Mrs Gaskell was at pains to emphasise the near-unbridgeable gulf between employers and employees, and their inability to communicate with each other. A great contrast is provided in the latter part of *North and South* in her portrayal of the intercourse which develops between Thornton and his men, and the acknowledgement of their mutual dependence. This change probably represents Elizabeth Gaskell's belief in the possibility of progress through more contact on a personal level, an optimistic but somewhat unrealistic outlook.

Whilst the industrial theme is central, and is also used to highlight the differences between Margaret and Thornton, the theme of personal integrity is also crucial to the novel. Margaret is presented as a dignified, upright, honest, sincere girl; there are frequent references to her regal presence and to her fearless belief in openness and truthfulness. It is, therefore, ironic that she becomes deeply involved in deception, feels cornered into lying and, because of the danger to Frederick, is unable to justify herself. She persuades him to consult Henry Lennox, in order to try and clear his name:

'You disobeyed authority — that was bad; but to have stood

by, without word or act, while that authority was brutally used, would have been infinitely worse. People know what you did; but not the motives that elevate it out of a crime into an heroic protection of the weak.' (p. 326)

This course of action results in the episode at Outwood Station where, in the first place, Thornton sees her (and so knows of her presence and subsequent lie) and, in the second place, the unfortunate contretemps occurs with Leonards, the former sailor. All these coincidences, including Thornton's later involvement as a magistrate, strike the reader as somewhat unlikely, but we have previously seen Mrs Gaskell's predilection for implausible coincidences; for example, in *Cranford*, the Brunonis' encounter with Aga Jenkyns in India; and in *Ruth*, Mr Donne, the parliamentary candidate, being none other than Ruth's seducer, Mr Bellingham.

The reader is partly prepared for Margaret's lie by the very insistence on her integrity, and also by Bessy's remark: '"I wonder how she'll sin. All on us must sin."' (p. 188), but the horror with which she herself views her sin is used to good effect, and emphasises the value Elizabeth Gaskell put on personal integrity: she suffers for her deception as Thurstan Benson did for his in *Ruth*. In addition, her despair at Thornton's knowledge of her lie makes clear to the reader, and eventually to Margaret herself, how much she values his good opinion, and how important it is for her peace of mind. Thornton is indeed shocked that she should have 'stained her whiteness by a falsehood' (p. 351), and she feels that ' . . .in Mr Thornton's eyes she was degraded'. (p. 355) Long after leaving Milton, she worries about her lie, and eventually asks Mr Bell to tell Mr Thornton the truth. She dismisses Mr Bell's attempt to minimise her sin by telling him: '"It was wrong, disobedient, faithless' (p. 485), and states that: '"What other people may think of the rightness or wrongness is nothing in comparison to my own deep knowledge, my innate conviction that it was wrong."' (p. 487) When Mr Bell dies without having given the hoped-for explanation to Mr Thornton, she accepts that:

It was a just consequence of her sin, that all excuses for it, all temptation to it, should remain for ever unknown to the person in whose opinion it had sunk her lowest. She stood face to face at last with her sin. (p. 502)

Elizabeth Gaskell reverts again and again to her belief that honesty and integrity must not be compromised, and nowhere more insistently than in *North and South*. Mr Hale relinquishes his comfortable living in the Church of England because of his doubts; Thornton finally admits he was wrong in ignoring the general welfare of his workers, and is not prepared to speculate when trade is bad to try to save his business: '"Honest men are ruined by a rogue," he said gloomily. "As I stand now, my creditors' money is safe — every farthing of it."' He goes on to explain that, if his speculation were to succeed: '"I should be a rich man, and my peace of conscience would be gone!"' (p. 516) Margaret, who is constantly racked by guilt because of her lie, says on finally accepting Thornton: '"Oh, Mr Thornton, I am not good enough!"' (p. 529)

Much of the interest in *North and South* centres on the use of contrast; it is used even in the presentation of minor characters. Margaret's whining, self-centred mother is a perfect foil for the strong, unyielding mother of John Thornton. Mrs Hale never ceases to feel that her marriage to a country vicar was a come-down for her, the ward of Sir John Beresford, and is even more horrified than Margaret at having to live 'in the middle of factories and factory people!' (p. 80) Mrs Thornton, on the other hand, is portrayed as resolute, clear-headed, uncomplaining, proud of her son and of Milton with its factories and warehouses. She is a splendidly-drawn character, uncompromising and out-spoken. She tells Mr Hale that she disapproves of her son's studies:

'Classics may do very well for men who loiter away their lives in the country or in colleges; but Milton men ought to have their thoughts and powers absorbed in the work of to-day.' (p. 159)

Nevertheless, her pride in her son is movingly conveyed, as is her attitude towards her spiritless, vain daughter, Fanny, whom she smothers in tenderness so as to hide her real contempt for such a weak character. She is fiercely jealous of John's affections, but when she reluctantly accepts that he loves Margaret, she excites our sympathy as she unpicks her initials from the household linen, which she expects will now belong to a future daughter-in-law. She believes that: '"To be chosen by John, would separate a kitchen-wench from the rest of the world."' (p. 270) and grudgingly admits that Margaret possesses many of the characteristics she admires: frankness, pungency and spirit. Of course, when Margaret rejects her son, she feels great relief and indulges her vicious feelings towards Margaret for causing John such misery. We can well hear the indignant tone to which Margaret refers at the end of the book, when she imagines how Mrs Thornton will greet the news of John's forthcoming marriage to 'that woman!' Mrs Thornton's fierce pride, her deep love for her son, and her forthrightness are conveyed with economy and precision, a masterly characterisation.

It was not until she wrote *Wives and Daughters* that Mrs Gaskell was to display throughout a full-length novel the irony and humour which were so effective in *Cranford*. In *North and South*, however, the tone is lighter than in *Mary Barton*, and touches of humour are more frequently evident, especially in the portrayals of Fanny and Edith. Fanny is so terrified when an angry crowd gathers during the strike, that she locks her brother out in her 'mad flight', faints, and has to be carried by her mother to a safer place, and, when told that Margaret may be bleeding to death, makes the totally inadequate comment: '"Bleed! oh, how horrid! How has she got hurt?"' (p. 238). Afterwards, her only concern is with how terrified *she* has been and how sick and faint *she* has felt. Her brother views her with contempt and contrasts her unfavourably with Margaret:

'I see a great deal of difference between Miss Hale and Fanny. I can imagine that the one may have weighty reasons, which may and ought to make her overlook any seeming impropriety in her conduct. I never knew Fanny have weighty reasons for anything.' (p. 389)

And in a dismissive comment on Fanny's preparations for her forthcoming marriage, Mrs Gaskell tells us that:

Mr Thornton was only too glad to mark his grateful approbation of any sensible man, who could be captivated by Fanny's second-rate airs and graces, by giving her ample means for providing herself with the finery, which certainly rivalled, if it did not exceed, the lover in her estimation. (p. 441)

Edith also pays undue attention to appearance; she is very anxious about Margaret's attitude: '"Oh! I was afraid you'd dress in brown and dust-colour,"' (p. 509) she tells her. Edith's superficiality is satirised when she tells her brother-in-law that she would like him to marry Margaret because 'it would be so nice for us all', and 'I should always feel comfortable about the children, if I had Margaret settled down near me'. (p. 527)

Problems connected with the serialisation of *North and South* led to much ill-feeling between Mrs Gaskell and Dickens. However, she was pleased when he eventually wrote to congratulate her, for it is clear from her letters that she suffered considerable strain whilst writing it. The general favour with which *North and South* was received was probably due not only to her presenting the point of view of the masters as well as of the workers, and painting a more optimistic picture of relations between them, but also to the over-riding concern of the book with the slowly developing relationship between two characters at first so antagonistic to each other.

Notes

1. Hopkins, *Elizabeth Gaskell, her Life and Work*, p. 137.
2. Ibid., p. 138.
3. Jane Austen, *Pride and Prejudice*, chap. 34.
4. Ibid., chap. 56.
5. John Donne, *Devotions*.
6. *Mary Barton*, p. 221.

Heaven her people would keep a little firmer on their legs,'
Dickens wrote,[2] although in a different connection.

The story is set in three main areas: London, rural Hampshire
and the industrial north. It opens in a prosperous home in
Harley Street, where Margaret has grown up with her Aunt Shaw
and Cousin Edith. After Edith's marriage (at the end of the first
chapter), Margaret returns to her parents' home in the beautiful
hamlet of Helstone in Hampshire; it is 'like a village in a poem',
Margaret comments. (p. 42) The next few chapters paint a loving
picture of these surroundings as seen through Margaret's eyes.
But her stay there lasts only a few months, for her father, the
vicar of Helstone, faces up to the fact that he can no longer accept
all the tenets of the established Church of England, and must
therefore resign his living. He fixes on Milton Northern (Manchester) as the future home for the family, as he will be able to
earn a living there as tutor to several of the manufacturers.

The contrast in setting, when the Hale family moves to Milton
Northern, with its smoke, grime, noise and crowded tumult, is
vividly evoked. Mr and Mrs Hale and Margaret, together with
their faithful middle-aged servant, Dixon, begin their new life in
this fast-growing industrial town, so different from anything they
have previously known. Mrs Hale, Dixon and Margaret are all at
first deeply prejudiced against the town and its inhabitants; in
Margaret's case, this is particularly expressed through her dis-
dain for the views of her father's chief and favourite pupil, John
Thornton, a mill-owner.

Soon after they settle in Milton, Mrs Hale's health begins to
deteriorate; she blames this on the environment, although she is,
in fact, suffering from an incurable disease. Meanwhile, Margaret
becomes involved in an ugly scene at Thornton's house, where
she has gone on an errand. A crowd of strikers, incensed because
Thornton has imported unskilled Irish knob-sticks to break the
strike, begins to hurl missiles at him; Margaret interposes herself
and is struck by a stone. The crowd disperses, but Thornton, who
over the course of the preceding months has come to admire
Margaret immensely, is encouraged by her action to propose to
her; he is haughtily refused. Later, Frederick, Margaret's elder
brother, who is living in Spain because of the threat of court-
martial if he returns to England, comes back secretly to visit his
dying mother. On his leaving Milton, he and Margaret are seen

adapt her writing to these external requirements. Although a considerable amount of her work was published in periodicals, it is significant that only two full-length novels, *North and South* and *Wives and Daughters*, appeared first in this form.

Inevitably, one compares *North and South* with *Mary Barton*, its predecessor on an industrial theme; however, apart from the fact that the main setting in each novel is an industrial town based on Manchester, the differences are more striking than the similarities. *North and South* has an assurance and confidence of style which are the mark of a much more experienced writer. Authorial comment is not, as in *Mary Barton* and *Ruth*, so obviously interspersed throughout the text, but is, in the main, implicit in the actions and words of the characters, although the subtle irony and humour which the writer was to display to great effect in *Wives and Daughters* was already evident at this stage. One obvious difference is the much more sympathetic presentation of the 'masters' in *North and South* than in *Mary Barton*, and certainly the later novel did not provoke the ill-feeling and controversy that the earlier one had done. It would, however, be a mistake to assume that the more sympathetic portrayal of the mill-owners was an attempt to placate any of the previous hostile response; the life of the 'hands' is still shown as hard, and Mrs Gaskell did not hesitate to expose any injustices she saw in the actions of the mill-owners. As she matured, she became increasingly aware that it was not a simple matter of black and white, but that there were many subtle shades of grey on both sides, and this understanding is evident, especially as personified in the mill-owner, John Thornton, and the mill-hand, Nicholas Higgins. In any case, her main concern is with the developing perception and feelings of the two main characters, Margaret Hale and John Thornton; and the industrial aspect of the novel, whilst it cannot be separated from this, is subordinate to it and is largely used to illustrate how this empathy develops.

Elizabeth Gaskell originally called the novel 'Margaret Hale', but Dickens suggested 'North and South'; this was accepted, albeit reluctantly, by the author. She wrote to him: 'I think a better title than N. & S. would have been "Death & Variations". There are 5 deaths, each beautifully suited to the character of the individual.' (L. 220) Five deaths are described in the novel, but in fact, including Mrs Boucher, six characters in all die. 'I wish to

6 A Fitting Tribute: *The Life of Charlotte Brontë*

> 'The work is now done, and done rightly, as I wished it to be.'
>
> Rev. Patrick Brontë[1]

Elizabeth Gaskell and Charlotte Brontë first met in August 1850 at the Windermere house of their mutual friends, Sir James and Lady Kay-Shuttleworth. They had both previously shown an interest in each other: Charlotte had sent a copy of her novel *Shirley* to Mrs Gaskell in November 1849, the month after its publication and, a few months before their meeting, Elizabeth Gaskell had written to Lady Kay-Shuttleworth: 'To return to Miss Brontë; I should like to know her very much'. (L. 72) Elizabeth Gaskell's poise and pleasant social ease contrasted greatly with Charlotte Brontë's shyness and fear of strangers, but there was an immediate rapport between them; this formed the basis of their mutual esteem and deep friendship, which lasted until Charlotte's unexpected and untimely death in March 1855.

In the biography Mrs Gaskell quotes from one of her own letters, giving her first impressions of Charlotte Brontë:

She is (as she calls herself) *undeveloped*, thin, and more than half a head shorter than I am; soft brown hair, not very dark; eyes (very good and expressive, looking straight and open at you) of the same colour as her hair; a large mouth; the forehead square, broad, and rather overhanging. She has a very sweet voice; rather hesitates in choosing her expressions, but when chosen they seem without an effort admirable, and just befitting the occasion; there is nothing overstrained, but perfectly simple. (pp. 417–18)

Several succeeding letters are full of this meeting, of further descriptions and of what she had learnt from Charlotte about her hard, sad life. This obviously made a profound impression on

Elizabeth Gaskell, whose understanding and sympathy must have encouraged Charlotte to talk about her early life, her family and her writing. Mrs Gaskell wrote to her friend, Eliza Fox: 'Miss Brontë *is* a nice person. . . . She is quiet sensible unaffected with high noble aims', (L. 79) and later in the same letter she explains:

> She is sterling and true; and if she is a little bitter she checks herself, and speaks kindly and hopefully of things and people directly; the wonder to me is how she can have kept heart and power alive in her life of desolation.

A month after this meeting, Charlotte Brontë wrote to Miss Wooler, her lifelong friend, who had formerly been her headmistress and employer:

> You say that you suspect I have formed a large circle of acquaintance by this time. No: I cannot say that I have. I doubt whether I possess either the wish or the power to do so. A few friends I should like to have, and these few I should like to know well. (p. 420)

This must surely apply to the newly-formed, burgeoning friendship with Mrs Gaskell, with whom she was already in correspondence. In June 1851 Charlotte, on her way home from a month-long visit to London, paid her first visit to the Gaskells in Manchester. In a letter to Mr Smith, her publisher, she refers to her Manchester visit and makes clear her admiration for Elizabeth Gaskell and her pleasure in their friendship:

> The visit to Mrs Gaskell on my way home let me down easily; though I spent only two days with her they were very pleasant. She lives in a large, cheerful, airy house, quite out of Manchester smoke; a garden surrounds it, and, as in this hot weather the windows were kept open, a whispering of leaves and a perfume of flowers always pervaded the rooms. Mrs Gaskell herself is a woman of whose conversation and company I should not soon tire. She seems to me kind, clever, animated, and unaffected; her husband is a good and kind man too.[2]

In April 1853 Charlotte again stayed with the Gaskells, this they lead out of the mills.' (p. 168)

Margaret finds this hard to accept; she lectures Thornton on the theme of: 'No man is an Island, entire of itself',[5] telling him that:

' . . . you are a man, dealing with a set of men over whom you have, whether you reject the use of it or not, immense power, just because your lives and your welfare are so constantly and intimately interwoven. God has made us so that we must be mutually dependent.' (p. 169)

But, whilst Mrs Gaskell presents most of Margaret's views sympathetically, it is clear that she respects the proud independence of the people of Darkshire (Lancashire) in wanting to manage without the charity of outsiders. When Margaret gives some money to Bessy for her neighbours, the Bouchers, a large family suffering considerable hardship during the strike, Bessy tells her that:

'Yo're not to think we'd ha' letten 'em clem, for all we're a bit pressed oursel'; if neighbours doesn't see after neighbours, I dunno who will.' Bessy seemed almost afraid lest Margaret should think they had not the will, and, to a certain degree, the power of helping one whom she evidently regarded as having a claim upon them. (p. 208)

This is a very different attitude from the one Margaret is used to in Hampshire, where the poor cottagers gratefully accept handouts from those higher up the social ladder than themselves.

Money (as in the Drumble outlook in *Cranford*) is considered in Milton as the keystone of human relationships. When John Thornton tries to temper his mother's dislike of Margaret, she retorts: 'You're never thinking of marrying her? — a girl without a penny'. (p. 193) and Bessy explains to Margaret that people 'thinken a deal o' money here; and I reckon yo've not getten much'. (p. 199) Margaret experiences difficulty in finding a servant to help Dixon, for 'Mr Hale was no longer looked upon as Vicar of Helstone, but as a man who only spent at a certain rate'. (p. 109) and Margaret, who has despised trade and 'shoppy people', has to accept that her family is viewed with suspicion

From that day Milton became a brighter place to her. It was not the long, bleak sunny days of spring, nor yet was it that time was reconciling her to the town of her habitation. It was that in it she had found a human interest. (p. 113)

When she later visits Bessy, she begins to respond to the town in a way which was doubtless similar to that in which Mrs Gaskell herself had responded to Manchester:

As she went along the crowded narrow streets, she felt how much of interest they had gained by the simple fact of her having learnt to care for a dweller in them. (p. 143)

Thornton's attitude is exemplified in his treatment of his workmen, or 'hands', a term which he uses naturally, but which Margaret dislikes. He does not, and will not, explain to the men his decisions in running the mill, including his refusal to raise wages. This results in a strike, an important episode in the novel, all of which is reminiscent of *Mary Barton*. Margaret cannot accept this high-handed treatment of the men:

'But why,' asked she, 'could you not explain what good reason you have for expecting a bad trade?' . . .
'Do you give your servants reasons for your expenditure, or your economy in the use of your own money? We, the owners of capital, have a right to choose what we will do with it.'
'A human right,' said Margaret, very low. (p. 164)

Again, when there is a potential riot outside Thornton's house, Margaret goads him into facing his angry workmen:

'Speak to your workmen as if they were human beings. Speak to them kindly. . . . If you have any courage or noble quality in you, go out and speak to them, man to man!' (p. 232)

An essential concomitant of Thornton's attitude is that he respects the independence of his men outside working hours:

'And I say, that the masters would be trenching on the independence of their hands, in a way that I, for one, should not feel justified in doing, if we interfered too much with the life

(*above*) Haworth Church and Parsonage in 1857, drawing by Elizabeth
Gaskell (*below*) Charlotte Brontë in 1850, drawing by George
Richmond

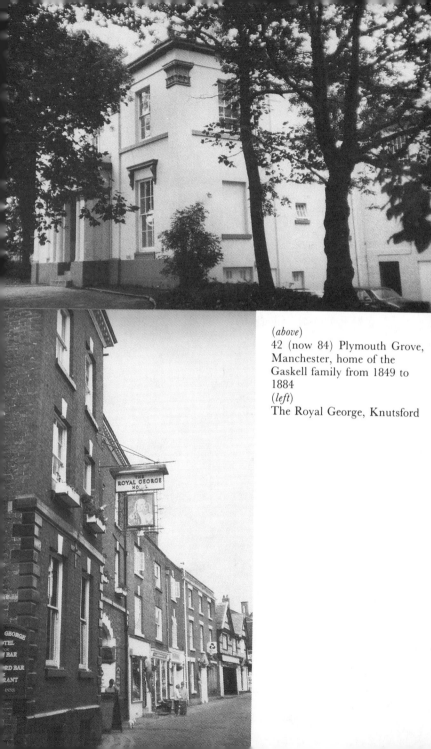

(*above*)
42 (now 84) Plymouth Grove, Manchester, home of the Gaskell family from 1849 to 1884
(*left*)
The Royal George, Knutsford

together at the railway station by Thornton who, completely unaware of Frederick's identity, assumes he is Margaret's lover, and is extremely jealous, and also puzzled by this apparently clandestine meeting. In addition, Frederick is recognised by a former sailor, who tries to denounce him, so as to get the reward. Frederick gives him a push, and the man falls. He dies a few days later, although the extent to which Frederick's actions are responsible for his death is never made completely clear. However, the police become involved and, in order to protect Frederick, Margaret denies that she was present at the scene. To her chagrin, Mr Thornton learns of her lie, and this becomes a source of extreme concern to her, for her feelings towards him are gradually changing, and she is increasingly anxious about losing his good opinion.

Since living in Milton, Margaret has also become involved with the family of a mill-hand, Nicholas Higgins, and especially with his daughter, Bessy, who later dies of tuberculosis, so that we learn about the lives of a worker's family as well as that of a manufacturer. After the death of his wife, Mr Hale ages rapidly, and dies suddenly whilst visiting his great friend, Margaret's godfather, Mr Bell, in Oxford. Margaret, now without any reason to remain in Milton, returns to Harley Street, where it happens that the Shaw family has just returned after an absence abroad of three years. John Thornton and Margaret Hale do not expect to meet again, so the possibility of a further open declaration of his deep feeling for her, and of her fast-developing appreciation and tenderness for him appears most unlikely. However, Margaret unexpectedly becomes his landlord, for Mr Bell dies and leaves his fortune, including much property in Milton, to her. Thornton is just now beset by financial problems, and decides he must close down his mill. He goes to London to settle various matters, including the lease of his property, with Margaret's financial adviser, Henry Lennox. Margaret proposes a business arrangement to Thornton, namely, to lend him the money to continue working his mill, and this precipitates the conventional happy ending.

North and South has been criticised for its extremely slow opening; as Martin Dodsworth points out in his preface to the Penguin edition: 'The novel starts three times — in Harley Street, in Helstone, and in Milton — and only really gets under way at the third attempt.' (p. 12) What, then, is the purpose of the two apparently halting starts? Firstly, what is the purpose of the first chapter set in the midst of wealthy London society? *North and South*, as its title conveys, is much concerned with contrast, and the life-style portrayed in the opening scene provides a startling contrast to Margaret's later life in Milton Northern. In addition, Margaret is a complete contrast to her pretty, delicately soft, fairy-tale cousin. Edith is compared to Titania: ' . . . dressed in white muslin and blue ribbons', and to 'a soft ball of muslin and ribbon, and silken curls' (p. 35), and to Sleeping Beauty. (p. 40) She has 'beautiful Indian shawls and scarfs' (p. 37) which have a 'spicy Eastern smell' (p. 39), and there is even a reference to Cinderella, which suggests that Edith, for whom 'the course of true love. . .had run remarkably smooth' (p. 37), is about to marry her 'tall, handsome' prince! Margaret is presented as a deeper, more interesting character; even physically, with her 'tall, finely made figure', she is contrasted with Edith, and we learn that she longs for the simplicity and quietness of her parents' home, to which she is about to return. 'The idea of stately simplicity accords well with your character' (p. 42), Henry Lennox tells her, and we see examples also of her practicality and helpfulness. So, even by the end of the first chapter, the heroine is emerging as a girl with depth to her character, who is about to return to a world very different from that of the Harley Street drawing-room. The novel in fact closes in the same drawing-room, and the contrast between the young, inexperienced Margaret of the opening and the mature woman, who has passed through so much sorrow and deep feeling, is highlighted by the use of the same setting, and provides further justification for opening the novel at this point and in this way.

The following few chapters set in Helstone also provide a striking contrast with the main setting of Milton Northern; they portray another aspect of the South which has up to now formed the background to Margaret's life. From these chapters we learn not only about the natural beauty of the South compared with the man-made ugliness of the North, but also about the paternalistic attitude of the gentry, which contrasts with that of the Milton manufacturers, who show no concern about the living conditions of their workers. The chapters set in Helstone also enable Mrs Gaskell to introduce and develop the religious theme which is woven into the story, although it is actually of less significance well-spread breakfast-table', where 'they lazily enjoyed their nicely prepared food.' (p. 107) He is treated kindly, but without any understanding of the urgency of the situation, and he is given an out-patient order only for several days ahead.

This inability of the rich to understand the desperation of the poor is a theme recurring throughout the novel. The gap between them is enormous, both materially and emotionally; the rich have no conception of the crushing poverty which breaks the spirit of a man watching his children literally 'clemming' (starving) to death. Mrs Gaskell underlines this by referring on two occasions to the parable of Dives and Lazarus in the Book of Luke. Dives is the man who enjoys wealth and great material comfort on earth, whilst Lazarus, the beggar, suffers on earth, living only on the crumbs from the rich man's table. In the next world, however, Lazarus is rewarded in Heaven, whilst Dives is tormented in Hell. There is a gulf between them which cannot be crossed. So John Barton, when we first meet him expounding his beliefs to George Wilson during the relatively happy outing to Green Heys Field, says:

'We are their slaves as long as we can work; we pile up their fortunes with the sweat of our brows; and yet we are to live as separate as if we were in two worlds; ay, as separate as Dives and Lazarus, with a great gulf betwixt us . . .' (p. 45)

and later, after the abortive attempt to present the Charter to parliament:

'Ay, London's a fine place,' said he, 'and finer folk live in it than I ever thought on, or ever heerd tell on except in th' story-books. They are having their good things now, that afterwards they may be tormented.'

whilst the author comments: 'Still at the old parable of Dives and Lazarus! Does it haunt the minds of the rich as it does those of the poor?' (p. 142)

Throughout the story, Mrs Gaskell has interwoven the theme of people's inability to communicate with each other, and there-fore to understand each other's motives and attitudes. This inability is sometimes caused by sheer ignorance of another's

21

situation; perhaps if Mr Carson or his son had visited the Davenports, and seen the appalling conditions in which they were living, they might have acted with a greater sense of urgency, a truer understanding of the fearful situation, for young Harry Carson is moved enough to give Wilson five shillings for 'the poor fellow', whilst his father, when he finally visits the Bartons' home to hear John's confession of murdering Harry, is forcibly struck, on returning home, by:

> . . . the grinding squalid misery he had remarked in every part of John Barton's house, and which contrasted strangely with the pompous sumptuousness of the room in which he now sat. Unaccustomed wonder filled his mind at the reflection of the different lots of the brethren of mankind. (p. 439)

The failure in communication is caused by haughtiness, by a wilful disregard and neglect of the feelings and understanding of others, particularly those considered inferiors. So, when the men are striking because of want and need:

> No one thought of treating the workmen as brethren and friends, and openly, clearly, as appealing to reasonable men, stating the exact and full circumstances, which led the masters to think it was the wise policy of the time to make sacrifices themselves, and to hope for them from the operatives. (p. 232)

Perhaps the gulf between the two sides would still have remained, even if the masters had tried to explain the position clearly to the workmen, but it might have been narrowed, for the masters, without intimate experience of the overwhelming conditions in which the poor exist, fail again and again to understand the situation. Even Mr Carson, towards the end of the story, and after seeing where and how John Barton lived, could say (in trying to explain his position to Job and Jem):

> 'We cannot regulate the demand for labour. No man or set of men can do it. It depends on events which God alone can control. When there is no market for our goods, we suffer just as much as you can do.' (p. 456)

and provokes mild Job Legh into replying:

to ask him for forgiveness. John is horrified at the sight of the man and at his shrieks of pain and misery: '" . . . I, for one" he says, "ha' seen enough of what comes of attacking knob-sticks, and I'll ha' nought to do with it no more."' (p. 240) He develops his thoughts further and tells his fellow-members of the deputation:

> '. . . since I've thought on th' matter to-day, I've thought we han all on us been more like cowards in attacking the poor like ourselves; them as has none to help, but mun choose between vitriol and starvation.' (p. 241)

Towards the end of the book both John and Mr Carson learn a little about each other's attitudes and way of life, and so narrow and fleetingly bridge the gap between them, especially as individuals. John, filled with guilt at the murder he has committed, tries to explain to Mr Carson:

> 'Sir, one word! My hairs are grey with suffering, and yours with years — '
> 'And have I had no suffering?' asked Mr Carson, as if appealing for sympathy, even to the murderer of his child. (p. 434)

Mr Carson goes on to explain how much he has lost in the loss of his son, and succeeds in making John Barton understand:

> The eyes of John Barton grew dim with tears. Rich and poor, masters and men, were then brothers in the deep suffering of the heart; for was not this the very anguish he had felt for little Tom, in years so long gone by that they seemed like another life! (p. 435)

Tom, Barton's son, had died for lack of nourishment as a young lad long before the story opens, at a time when John had been laid off from his mill. There is a brief, melodramatic description of John seeing the wife of his employer coming from a shop of 'edible luxuries', carrying her purchases for a party, and 'Barton returned home with a bitter spirit of wrath in his heart, to see his only boy a corpse!' (p. 61) So John Barton is able to understand the feelings of another man on the loss of his son, a man with whom he previously thought he had nothing in common, to

'Not as much, I'm sure, sir; though I'm not given to Political Economy, I know that much. I'm wanting in learning, I'm aware; but I can use my eyes. I never see the Masters getting thin and haggard for want of food; I hardly ever see them making much change in their way of living, though I don't doubt they've got to do it in bad times. But it's in things for show they cut short; while for such as me, it's in things for life we've to stint.' (p. 456)

Another instance of the inability to communicate, this time on a personal level, occurs when Esther tries to warn John of Mary's liaison with Harry Carson; as a result of her own sufferings, she is very much aware of the life which will face Mary if she yields to the temptation of living unmarried with Harry, and she desperately wants to prevent this. In this case John, who is blindly prejudiced against Esther, refuses to listen, and flings her into the gutter, from where she is picked up by the police. Her half-delirious moans throughout the night centre around her failure to communicate her message to John: '"He would not listen to me; what can I do? He would not listen to me, and I wanted to warn him!"' (p. 170)

So, in both work and personal relationships, Elizabeth Gaskell emphasises the misunderstandings between, and the resulting separateness of, people — their lack of empathy. On the industrial front the lack of perception exists not only between masters and men, but even between different groups of desperate workers. Over the years John Barton changes, often for the worse, as he becomes more embittered and intransigent, but he also on occasion learns about his fellow-men and becomes more sympathetic towards them. This happens when he goes to visit a 'knob-stick', a strike-breaker, in hospital. The action of the knob-sticks, in working for lower wages, and thus ruining the effectiveness of the strike, has incensed many of the strikers, and there is much bitter feeling, often erupting in violence, including one particularly brutal form of action: throwing vitriol at the knob-sticks. One of John's fellow-workers is in gaol for throwing vitriol in a knob-stick's face and, because he is haunted by the sight of the man he has injured, he asks John to sell a silver watch which belonged to his mother, to give the money to the knob-stick for his family and time for a week, and it is clear that during these visits she became fond of the Gaskell children, especially Julia, who would have been under five on the first occasion. Charlotte was not naturally attracted to children, and the impression made on her by Mrs Gaskell's daughters helps to emphasise the happy atmosphere of the household and the considerable charm which the girls, as well as their mother, displayed.

In the following September Mrs Gaskell visited Haworth as Charlotte's guest, a sign of great favour. In two long letters (L. 166 and L. 167) written just after this, she describes the countryside, the house, Mr Brontë, the two servants, and the graveyard where so many of the Brontës were buried. Above all, she depicts Charlotte's present way of life, much of what she learnt about Charlotte's earlier life, and about her attitudes and temperament. The visit provided a fund of information, on which she was later to draw extensively. It also laid the basis for Mr Brontë's respect for Mrs Gaskell and his subsequent dependence on her ability as his daughter's biographer. The intimacy which developed between the two women made a deep impression on Charlotte too, and she wrote to her guest:

After you left, the house felt very much as if the shutters had been suddenly closed and the blinds let down. One was sensible during the remainder of the day of a depressing silence, shadow, loss and want.[3]

The final meeting between the two friends took place in May 1854, when Charlotte spent three days in Manchester prior to her marriage to the Reverend Arthur Nicholls, her father's curate. Mrs Gaskell's busy life, and also her fear that Mr Nicholls would not approve of Charlotte's dissenting friends, put obstacles in the way of their meeting soon after the marriage, and then came Charlotte's sudden illness and death. In replying to a letter informing her of this, Elizabeth Gaskell wrote:

You may well say you have lost your best friend; strangers might know her by her great fame, but we loved her dearly for her goodness, truth and kindness, & those lovely qualities she carried with her where she is gone. (L. 232)

A few days later, she wrote to the same friend (Mr Greenwood, the Haworth stationer, who supplied the Brontë sisters with paper for their writing): "Dear, dear Miss Brontë. I wish I could do anything in my power for those whom she has loved, and left behind her!" (L. 233)

At the beginning of June 1855, two months after Charlotte's death, in a letter to the publisher, George Smith, Mrs Gaskell mentioned that she would like to:

> . . . put down everything I remembered about this dear friend and noble woman, before its vividness had faded from my mind: but I *know* that Mr Brontë, and I *fear* that Mr Nicholls, would not like this made public. (L. 242)

However, within a fortnight, she received a request from Mr Brontë to write a biography of his daughter. She again wrote to George Smith to tell him of this and of her response:

> I have received (most unexpectedly) the enclosed letter from Mr Brontë; I have taken some time to consider the request made in it, but I have consented to write it, *as well as I can*. Of course it becomes a more serious task than the one which, as you know, I was proposing to myself, to put down my personal recollections &c, with no intention of immediate publication, — if indeed of publication at all. I shall have now to omit a good deal of detail as to her home, and the circumstances, which must have had so much to do in forming her character. All these can be merely indicated during the life-time of her father, and to a certain degree in the lifetime of her husband — Still I am very anxious to perform this grave duty laid upon me well and fully. Of course it strengthens my determination to go over to Haworth as now I *must* see Mr Brontë. (L. 245)

The visit referred to in this letter took place in July, and, immediately after leaving Haworth, Mrs Gaskell wrote to Ellen Nussey, a lifelong friend of Charlotte Brontë, to request as much information as possible about Charlotte. (She in fact received over 350 of Charlotte's letters from Miss Nussey.) From this letter we learn of Mr Brontë's 'impetuous wish' that a biography should be written, and of Mr Nicholls's reluctance. She also tells us that Mr Brontë's last words to her that day were: 'No quailing

Mrs Gaskell! no drawing back!' (L. 257) and she certainly carried out the commission with the hard work, determination and single-mindedness so evident in all she undertook. Many of her extant letters written during the time she was writing the biography are filled with enquiries for material; she obviously searched out and read all available material with thoroughness, and visited all the places where Charlotte had lived, including Brussels.

Many of the qualities which characterise Mrs Gaskell's work as a novelist are evident in the biography. From the outset we are aware of her concern with setting; she describes Keighley, the town nearest to Haworth, the district between Keighley and Haworth, and the first impression made on a visitor approaching Haworth:

> Right before the traveller on this road rises Haworth village; he can see it for two miles before he arrives, for it is situated on the side of a pretty steep hill, with a background of dun and purple moors, rising and sweeping away yet higher than the church, which is built at the very summit of the long narrow street. All round the horizon there is this same line of sinuous wave-like hills; the scoops into which they fall only revealing other hills beyond, of similar colour and shape, crowned with wild, bleak moors — grand, from the ideas of solitude and loneliness which they suggest, or oppressive from the feeling which they give of being pent-up by some monotonous and illimitable barrier, according to the mood of mind in which the spectator may be. (p. 55)

With similar minute detail we are told about Haworth parsonage, the home of the Brontës from 1820, when Charlotte was three. Mrs Gaskell then fills in the historical background of Haworth, the lives of Charlotte's parents up to the death of Mrs Brontë, and the subsequent arrival of her sister, Miss Branwell, to look after the family. She frequently uses a similar technique in her novels, giving the setting in broad sweeps, narrowing down to detailed description and then sketching in the background history of the main characters.

As in Mrs Gaskell's major novels, the heroine assumes the central position; the author is concerned with a full portrayal of her character, its strengths and its weaknesses. So we are shown how Charlotte Brontë's life helped to form and to highlight her character, her goodness predominating over any defects. As Alan Shelston points out in his introduction to the Penguin edition, Charlotte Brontë could have been a Gaskell heroine: a motherless girl, coping with full household responsibilities and a somewhat eccentric, difficult father for whom she shows unswerving affection; she faces her trials with fortitude and determination, but occasionally rebels against difficulties; she matures into a woman of integrity, exhibiting selfless devotion in the face of sickness and death. Such an outline could describe the lives of Mary Barton, Margaret Hale, Molly Gibson and even, to some extent, of Ruth Hilton.

In the early chapters, we learn something of Mr Brontë's eccentric behaviour: for example, how he burnt some of the children's boots because 'they were too gay and luxurious for his children' (p. 89) and how he cut into shreds a silk gown belonging to his wife for a similar reason. He was given to bursts of temper, which he worked off by firing pistols out of the back-door in rapid succession, or on one occasion by burning the hearth-rug, and on another by sawing the backs off some chairs. Mrs Gaskell tells us:

> I have named these instances of eccentricity in the father because I hold the knowledge of them to be necessary for a right understanding of the life of his daughter. (p. 90)

We may assume that she carefully selected and possibly softened these incidents, so as to cause Mr Brontë as little offence as possible.

She next focuses more intensively on the Brontë sisters, especially Charlotte. The most important early episode is connected with the Cowan's Bridge School for the Daughters of Clergymen. Charlotte's two elder sisters, Maria and Elizabeth, went there in July 1824, and two months later Mr Brontë sent the next two girls, Charlotte and Emily. Mrs Gaskell was concerned (when, in her judgement, it was possible) to present a full and accurate picture of Charlotte's life, but she was aware that in writing about this school, the inspiration for Lowood School in *Jane Eyre*, she was on dangerous ground:

I now come to a part of my subject which I find great difficulty in treating, because the evidence relating to it on each side is so conflicting that it seems almost impossible to arrive at the truth. Miss Brontë more than once said to me, that she should not have written what she did of Lowood in 'Jane Eyre', if she had thought the place would have been so immediately identified with Cowan's Bridge, although there was not a word in her account of the institution but what was true at the time when she knew it. (p. 98)

Many of the problems (familiar to readers of *Jane Eyre*), which beset the pupils are depicted; for example, the repulsive food and the long, unsheltered walk to the damp, bitterly cold church. A fever did in fact break out at the school, but the Brontë sisters escaped it. However, Maria and Elizabeth, their already poor health deteriorating even more rapidly, no doubt owing to the conditions at the school, died in 1825; this great loss and shock certainly coloured Charlotte's attitude to the school. The family of the Reverend Carus Wilson, the founder of the school, threatened Mrs Gaskell with legal action after the publication of the biography and, as a result, she extensively revised the relevant chapter for the third edition. The text of the Penguin edition is that of the original, but the two revised chapters (Volume I, Chapters 4 and 13) appear in an appendix at the end of the book. To portray the harsh conditions experienced by Charlotte at the school was a necessary part of Mrs Gaskell's technique for showing the close interaction between environment and character; she included what in her opinion was an accurate and balanced account of the conditions existing when Charlotte attended the school, but she had to modify her comments in view of the protests following publication.

The remaining chapters in the first volume (the biography is divided into two volumes, each containing fourteen chapters) are concerned with Charlotte's later schooling at Miss Wooler's, her subsequent employment as a teacher at that school, with the early attempts at writing by the three remaining sisters, Charlotte, Emily and Anne, and their brother, Branwell. We also learn of Charlotte's experiences as a governess, of the sisters' plans for a school of their own, and of Charlotte's stay in Brussels, accompanied at first by Emily. We are told of the death of Miss

Branwell, of the abandonment of the school plan, and of the early stages of Branwell's deterioration. In the last chapter of this volume, we learn of the publication of poems by the three sisters under the pseudonyms of Currer, Ellis and Acton Bell.

Charlotte, like her biographer, was a prolific letter-writer, writing to her family when she herself was away from Haworth, and also to the few close friends she had, in particular Ellen Nussey and Miss Wooler. As she became well-known, her circle of correspondents increased, and included among others Thackeray, G.H. Lewes, Mrs Gaskell herself and Harriet Martineau. Many of her letters have survived; it was on these that Elizabeth Gaskell drew extensively, especially in the latter part of the biography. She emphasised this in a letter to George Smith:

> Now I am very careful what extracts I make; but still her language, where it can be used, is so powerful & living, that it would be a shame not to express everything that can be, in her own words. (L. 303)

About some episodes, however, there were no letters. Perhaps the most significant concerns Branwell's involvement with a Mrs Robinson; it forms the subject-matter of Volume I, Chapter 13, the second chapter which had to be rewritten because of the threat of legal action. Branwell was considered by his talented sisters as far more gifted than they, and Mr Brontë also 'did proud homage to the great gifts of his son'. (p. 153) But even as a young man of eighteen, Branwell exhibited 'many failings in moral conduct' (p. 153); this refers particularly to 'the undesirable distinction of having his company recommended by the landlord of the Black Bull to any chance traveller who might happen to feel solitary or dull over his liquor'. (p. 154) He never fulfilled his early promise and drifted through life. He became a clerk on the Leeds and Manchester railway, but was dismissed for negligence. He then became tutor to the family of à Mr Robinson in London, and her strictures on the relationship between Branwell and his employer's wife led Mrs Gaskell into serious trouble. She blamed Mrs Robinson (who had been widowed, and remarried, becoming Lady Scott, long before the biography was written) solely for Branwell's downfall. After being dismissed and forbidden to see Mrs Robinson again, Branwell returned home and told his side of the story to the family:

> . . . the blind father sat stunned, sorely tempted to curse the
> profligate woman, who had tempted his boy — his only son —
> into the deep disgrace of deadly crime. (p. 280)

Elizabeth Gaskell goes on to offer her own interpretation of the
relationship:

> The case presents the reverse of the usual features; the man
> became the victim; the man's life was blighted, and crushed
> out of him by suffering, and guilt entailed by guilt; the man's
> family were stung by keenest shame. The woman . . . goes
> flaunting about to this day in respectable society; a showy
> woman for her age; kept afloat by her reputed wealth. (p. 281)

We are told how, after her husband's death, Mrs Robinson
broke off all connection with Branwell, a condition imposed by
her husband if she was to benefit under his will. 'He [Branwell]
little knew how bad a depraved woman can be', comments Mrs
Gaskell. (p. 283) For the remaining years of his life, Branwell
drank to excess and took opium, suffering all the terrible consequences of these addictions, including delirium tremens.

In a letter to George Smith, Mrs Gaskell explains her reasons
for dealing so fully with this relationship, and for her strong
criticism of the former Mrs Robinson:

> . . .details of her life (past and present) which I heard from
> her own cousin. . .showed her to have been a bad heartless
> woman for long & long, — & to think of her going about
> calling, & dining out &c &c — (her own relations have been
> obliged to drop her acquaintance,) while those poor Brontës
> suffered so — for bad as Branwell was, — he was not absolutely
> ruined for ever, till she got hold of him, & he was not the first,
> nor the last. However, it is a horrid story, & I should not have
> told it but to show the life of prolonged suffering those Brontë
> girls had to endure. (L. 328)

We learn something of what they had to endure, and of Charlotte's
stoicism and resignation, from some of her letters quoted by
Mrs Gaskell:

We have not been very comfortable here at home lately. Branwell has, by some means, contrived to get more money from the old quarter, and has led us a sad life . . . Papa is harassed day and night; we have little peace; he is always sick; has two or three times fallen down in fits; what will be the ultimate end, God knows. But who is without their drawback, their scourge, their skeleton behind the curtain? It remains only to do one's best, and endure with patience what God sends. (p. 335)

After his death, Charlotte wrote:

Till the last hour comes, we never know how much we can forgive, pity, regret a near relative. All his vices were and are nothing now. We remember only his woes. (p. 352)

In keeping with her general purpose in the biography, Mrs Gaskell uses Branwell's problems to show the very great difficulties Charlotte had to face, and so demonstrate her sterling qualities in coping with them. The fact that Mrs Robinson's (Lady Scott's) name was not mentioned in the book was, she obviously assumed, sufficient to protect her from the laws of libel. However, the storm broke during her absence on the Continent, where she went immediately after she had delivered her manuscript. Mr Gaskell dealt with the matter in her absence, admitting that many of her original statements were based on insufficient information, apologising, and agreeing to retract them. On her return home, Mrs Gaskell was astonished at the furore caused by some parts of the biography. She wrote to Miss Nussey: 'I am in the Hornet's nest with a vengeance', and went on to explain that:

I *did so try* to *tell the truth*, & I believe *now* I hit as near the truth as any one *could* do. And I weighed every line with all my whole power & heart, so that every line should go to it's great purpose of making *her* known & valued, as one who had gone through such a terrible life with a brave & faithful heart. (L. 352)

Such difficulties may be considered the result of her acts of commission; there is, however, one glaring act of omission in the biography; this is the relationship between Charlotte and M. Héger, which Elizabeth Gaskell glosses over. Charlotte developed a strong passion for M. Héger during the time she spent in Brussels in his home and under his tuition. This was not reciprocated and eventually led to a breach between Charlotte and Madame Héger, who still felt so strongly about the episode almost fifteen years later, that she refused to meet Mrs Gaskell to talk about Charlotte. In order to spare the feelings of Charlotte's husband and father, and because she considered it did not reflect creditably on Charlotte herself, Mrs Gaskell played down the episode. She rationalised: 'the silent estrangement between Madame Héger and Miss Brontë' by referring to their religious differences:

> . . . the English Protestant's dislike of Romanism increased with her knowledge of it, and its effect upon those who professed it; and when occasion called for an expression of opinion from Charlotte Brontë, she was uncompromising truth. Madame Héger, on the opposite side, was not merely a Roman Catholic, she was *dévote*. (p. 263)

Mrs Gaskell must have been well aware of the truth. There is evidence that she saw four passionate letters written by Charlotte to M. Héger, and that she was worried about the posthumous publication of Charlotte's novel *The Professor*, for what it might reveal of Charlotte's attachment to Mr Héger. 'I dreaded lest the *Prof:* should involve anything with M. Héger — I had heard her say it related to her Brussels life.' (L. 308)

The second volume of the biography was not concerned with the kind of controversial issues covered in the first. It deals, on the personal side, with Mr Brontë's blindness and the ensuing successful operation, and with the illnesses and tragic deaths of Branwell, Emily and Anne, all within a year. This was followed for Charlotte by years of loneliness and isolation, during which she frequently suffered from very poor health. Then came the declaration by Mr Nicholls of his deep love for her, but her father strongly opposed the match, and Charlotte unselfishly yielded. Gradually, however, Mr Brontë became reconciled to the idea, and in June 1854 Mr Nicholls and Charlotte were married. There followed nine happy months, before Charlotte's health, always poor, and perhaps made worse by pregnancy at the age of thirty-eight, gave way entirely and in March 1855 she died:

Early on Saturday morning, March 31st, the solemn tolling of Haworth church-bell spoke forth the fact of her death to the villagers who had known her from a child, and whose hearts shivered within them as they thought of the two sitting desolate and alone in the old grey house. (p. 524)

Mrs Gaskell's skill in presenting the essentials simply, with economy and directness, are nowhere better illustrated than in the above quotation.

The other aspect of the second volume is Charlotte's literary success and rise to fame. At first she experienced difficulty, being unable to find a publisher for her first novel, *The Professor*. However, her second, *Jane Eyre*, was published in October 1847 and was favourably received. In December of that year, Emily's novel, *Wuthering Heights*, and Anne's, *Agnes Grey*, were published, but the sisters kept their identity quite secret. There was endless speculation as to the sex of Currer, Ellis and Acton Bell, and even whether they were actually three separate people. This impelled the sisters to prove that they were indeed three women; Charlotte and Anne went to London and presented themselves at the publishers, Smith, Elder, to show who they were. This was the first of a number of visits Charlotte made to London, usually staying with the Smiths. She was a centre of attraction, and met many people of importance in the literary world. This was not easy for her, as she always found meeting strangers and exposure to publicity disagreeable, and frequently suffered severe sick headaches and extreme tiredness as a result. In spite of her loneliness at Haworth after the death of her sisters, and of an increasing tendency to depression and irritability whilst there, a life of seclusion was overall more congenial to her than the round of social engagements which were an inevitable part of a visit to London — an experience so much enjoyed by Mrs Gaskell, following her own success as a novelist. Charlotte continued writing: *Shirley* and *Villette* were published in 1849 and 1853 respectively.

In closing her biography, Mrs Gaskell writes:

I appeal to that larger and more solemn public, who know how to look with tender humility at faults and errors; how to admire generously extraordinary genius, and how to reverence with warm, full hearts all noble virtue. To that Public I commit the memory of Charlotte Brontë. (p. 526)

She was anxious to convey Charlotte's predominant goodness, her stoicism, self-sacrifice and worth; these qualities, all much admired by Elizabeth Gaskell, shine through her story of Charlotte Brontë's life.

Notes

1. Letter from Rev. Patrick Brontë to Elizabeth Gaskell, in J. E. C. Welldon, 'The Brontë Family', *Cornhill Magazine*, April 1910.
2. Hopkins, *Elizabeth Gaskell, Her Life and Work*, p. 115.
3. Ibid., p. 164.

7 A Mixed Bag — Short Stories

> An honest tale speeds best being plainly told.
> Shakespeare: *Richard III*

During the whole period of her literary output, Elizabeth Gaskell was publishing short stories and novellas, from *The Three Eras of Libbie Marsh* in 1847 to *Cousin Phillis*, finished in 1864. That she had skill in telling a gripping tale is obvious from the fact that she never had difficulty in getting her stories published; indeed, they were often commissioned, particularly by Dickens, who usually paid generously for them.

These stories present some practical difficulties for the modern reader. In the first place, there are problems in getting hold of some of them, as there is no readily available complete edition. Secondly, in many cases they are much longer than the commonly accepted 'short story' of today, an important characteristic of which is surely that it can be conveniently read at a single sitting; this is frequently impractical with Elizabeth Gaskell's stories. The length may partly be explained by the serialisation of many of them in a variety of contemporary periodicals, and a further consequence of this is often evident in a lack of structure, for example, in *My Lady Ludlow*, *The Poor Clare* and *The Doom of the Griffiths*.

Many of the stories are concerned with themes and situations explored more fully in her novels: *Lizzie Leigh* deals with the plight of the unmarried mother; *Mr Harrison's Confessions* centres on life in the small community of Duncombe, which is reminiscent of Cranford; whilst the problem of the woman unwittingly committed to two lovers, which occurs in *The Manchester Marriage*, is developed in much greater depth in *Sylvia's Lovers*. She did not, however, restrict herself to such themes in these shorter works, but often ranged much more widely in both subject-matter and settings. Whilst *Sylvia's Lovers* is the only novel with an historical setting, quite a number of the shorter stories are set in the past; these include *My Lady Ludlow*, *Lois the Witch*, *An Accursed Race*, *The Doom of the Griffiths* and *The Squire's Story*. None of her novels is concerned with the supernatural, yet this is the theme of such stories as *The Old Nurse's Tale, Curious if True* and *The Poor Clare*. Rather than touch superficially on a great number of these tales, let us consider four in more detail, and from these appreciate some of her achievements and shortcomings in this field. *Half a Life-Time Ago* was published in October 1855, *My Lady Ludlow* between June and September 1858, *Lois the Witch* in October 1859 and *Cousin Phillis* between November 1863 and February 1864.

Half a Life-Time Ago tells the story of Susan Dixon, a strong-minded woman, who promises her dying mother to look after her younger brother, Will, who becomes seriously deranged after a bad dose of fever. Susan's lover, Michael Hurst, loathes Will and makes his confinement in a lunatic asylum a condition of marrying Susan. She does not hesitate to put her promise to her mother and love for her brother first and, as a result, she lives a hard, grim life, whilst Michael marries another local girl. He does not, however, prosper. When Will dies, Susan is left lonely and isolated. One November night, years later, she finds Michael buried in a snow-drift. With a superhuman effort she drags him to her home, but he is already dead. The following day, she goes to tell Michael's widow what has happened, and finally takes the widow and children to live with her.

The plot is simple enough, but the quality of this story lies in the finely-drawn character of Susan. We are made painfully aware of the suffering she experiences in giving up Michael for Will. After their final separation, she remembers poignantly places they had been to and things they had done together, and each evening she imagines she hears him approaching:

> She would wonder how she could have had strength, the cruel, self-piercing strength, to say what she had done; to stab herself with that stern resolution, of which the scar would remain till her dying day. It might have been right; but, as she sickened, she wished she had not instinctively chosen the right. (p. 89)

Her life with Willie is far from easy; he becomes increasingly violent, and she not only has to contend with this, but also, in order to prevent his being consigned to a madhouse, to keep his condition hidden:

The one idea of taking charge of him had deepened and deepened with years. It was graven into her mind as the object for which she lived. The sacrifice she had made for this object only made it more precious to her. (p. 92)

Her devotion to her mad brother is complete, and when he dies she experiences the worst fate of all: ' . . . there was no one left on earth for her to love'. (p. 93) She develops into a 'tall, gaunt, hard-featured, angular woman — who never smiled, and hardly ever spoke an unnecessary word. . .' (p. 60), whose home and farm are models of cleanliness and efficiency, but lack any human touch. She works tirelessly and uncomplainingly in her utter loneliness, having lost first Michael and then Will.

Mrs Gaskell achieves a moving but unsentimental ending by writing simply of Susan's change of life-style. There is a feeling of completeness, of the wheel coming full circle, in the apt conclusion to this story:

> When she returned to Yew Nook, she took Michael Hurst's widow and children with her to live there, and fill up the haunted hearth with living forms that should banish the ghosts.
> And so it fell out that the latter days of Susan Dixon's life were better than the former. (p. 102)

My Lady Ludlow is also notable for fine character drawing, in particular of Lady Ludlow herself and of Miss Galindo. There is present as well a little of the humour and sparkle of *Cranford*, but as Margaret Dawson, the narrator, explains: 'It is no story: it has, as I said, neither beginning, middle, nor end'. (p. 9) Within the tale is contained the story of Clément de Créquy, set in Paris during the French Revolution; this is a diffuse, irrelevant interlude, which could well have been developed into a separate story, but as it stands, it certainly endorses the claim that *My Lady Ludlow* is no story! Lady Ludlow, in whose home Margaret Dawson spends her adolescence, lives in Hanbury Court in Warwickshire. She is a small, dignified, elegant, old-fashioned lady, who rules her household and the local villagers on feudal principles; she is a firm believer in the distinctions of rank and class, and assumes that her judgement will be accepted, partly owing to her experience of life, but more especially because of her station in society. In particular, she deplores the idea of educating the 'lower orders':

> It was a right word. . .that I used, when I called reading and writing 'edge-tools'. If our lower orders have these edge-tools given to them, we shall have the terrible scenes of the French Revolution acted over again in England. (p. 59)

The boy who occasions these reflections, Harry Gregson, later breaks his thigh, and Lady Ludlow explains that: 'It all comes from over-education'. (p. 152) The story within a story about the French Revolution, in which two aristocrats are guillotined, is also used to illustrate the dangers of teaching the lower classes to read, for it is through this that the aristocrats are betrayed. But Lady Ludlow is shown gradually modifying her principles. We have seen that Susan Dixon is portrayed as both a stern upholder of moral behaviour and a woman of great compassion, and we find that Lady Ludlow, as she deals with individual instances, changes her attitude, so that her behaviour too is eventually both morally sound and humane. For example, at first she refuses to intercede on behalf of Job Gregson (Harry's father) who, she is told, has been wrongly committed to gaol for stealing; she has a stormy interview with the new parson, Mr Gray, refusing to accept his opinion, but as she finally admits: '"It so happened that I saw Job Gregson's wife and home — I felt that Mr Gray had been right and I had been wrong"'. (p. 40)

However, it takes her years to alter her views on education, but she does eventually withdraw her opposition to a village school, provided that:

> . . . the boys might only be taught to read and write, and the first four rules of arithmetic; while the girls were only to learn to read, and to add up in their heads, and the rest of the time to work at mending their own clothes, knitting stockings, and spinning. (p. 199)

Lady Ludlow is too wealthy, too influential and too much of an aristocrat to have fitted into Cranford society, but Miss Galindo would have been quite at home there. We are given a lengthy, rambling background history of Miss Galindo, although she only appears in the latter part of the story, when she comes as a clerk to help Lady Ludlow's steward. She is a poor gentlewoman, who keeps one servant: 'invariably chosen because she had some infirmity that made her undesirable to every one else'. (p. 129) She has a peppery temper, and delights in scolding her servants, who are nevertheless greatly attached to her. As she explains: ' "I must have something to stir my blood, or I should go off into an apoplexy; so I set to, and quarrel with Sally".' (p. 131) She tells us that as a young girl she thought of becoming an authoress, but after collecting paper, pens and ink

> . . . it ended in my having nothing to say, when I sat down to write. But sometimes, when I get hold of a book, I wonder why I let such a poor reason stop me. It does not others. (pp. 137–8)

Her inexhaustible kindness, talkativeness and wit add a much-needed sparkle to the second half of the tale.

Although Mrs Gaskell never visited the United States, the story of the Salem witch hunt of 1692 obviously fired her imagination, and she uses this setting for the story of young Lois Barclay. The actual episode, in which a fanatical delusion led to the arrest of hundreds and the eventual death of twenty, does indeed seem to have been precipitated by several young girls and an American-Indian servant in the house of the local pastor, elements which Mrs Gaskell weaves into her story of *Lois the Witch*. However, by introducing a young English girl, brought up happily and normally in an English country parsonage, into the household of her bigoted Puritan relations in Salem, their fanaticism and wildly emotional behaviour is highlighted.

It is a beautifully constructed, tautly-written story with no extraneous material. There is an inevitability in the outcome in which Lois, with no one to befriend or support her, is finally denounced as a witch, and hanged. From her very arrival in New England, Lois's thoughts are directed towards witchcraft; she even relates the story of old Hannah: ' . . . a poor, helpless, baited creature', who, in her home village of Barford, had cried out to Lois:

'Parson's wench, Parson's wench, yonder, in thy nurse's arms, thy dad hath never tried to save me, and none shall save thee when thou art brought up for a witch.' (p. 116)

The four relations with whom she goes to live in Salem are all depicted as somewhat abnormal. From her aunt, Grace Hickson, who 'had a kind of jealous dislike to her husband's English relations' (p. 122) she experiences 'positive, active antipathy to all the ideas Lois held most dear'. (p. 125) Grace comes to believe that Lois has bewitched her beloved son, Manasseh, and begs her to release him from the spell. When Lois protests her innocence, her aunt curses her most terribly and, throwing a handful of dust at her, leaves her to await execution the following morning.

The three cousins, Faith, Prudence and Manasseh, exhibit varying degrees of unbalance. Faith, at first the kindest and most sympathetic towards Lois, eventually becomes insanely jealous of her, believing she is her rival in love, and begins to think of her and refer to her as a witch. Prudence, portrayed as an impish child devoid of any feelings, behaves (according to the Indian servant, Nattee) as one possessed. It is she who finally, mercilessly, accuses Lois of witchcraft. The completely mad member of the family is Manasseh; he has had fits of insanity which his mother has kept secret, even having to tie him down with cords because of his violence. He believes he hears a voice telling him to 'Marry Lois!' and plagues her to agree to this. He admits that:

'At times I feel a creeping influence coming over me, prompting all evil thoughts and unheard-of deeds, and I question within myself, "Is not this the power of witchcraft?" and I sicken, and loathe all that I do or say, and yet some evil creature hath the mastery over me, and I must needs do and say what I loathe and dread.' (pp. 160–1)

Lois, a gentle, kind, loving, normal girl, is relentlessly swept along in this alien, fanatical environment by forces she can neither understand nor resist. The mass hysteria and inhumanity of the inhabitants of Salem form a poignant contrast with the well-balanced, warm-hearted young English girl, as her death draws inexorably nearer.

Mrs Gaskell's skill is revealed in this powerful, well-constructed story, in which all the elements blend convincingly, so that we are compelled to accept Lois as the foredoomed victim of the Salem delusion. Mrs Gaskell's love of justice is illustrated in the way she ends the story by including the historical fact that Judge Sewall acknowledged his error in 1713 and prayed publicly for forgiveness. However, as Hugh Lucy, Lois's English lover, truly says, 'All this will not bring my Lois to life again, or give me back the hope of my youth'. (p. 192)

In *Cousin Phillis*, which was written as a four-part serial, Mrs Gaskell returns to her Cheshire roots. She evokes the rural setting deliberately and carefully, and describes with poignancy Phillis Holman's deep love for Holdsworth, a clever, attractive railway engineer. Paul Manning, the narrator, is a distant cousin of Phillis; like Mary Smith in *Cranford*, he not only narrates, but also participates in the action, and it is he who introduces Holdsworth to the Holman family. He describes effectively the beauty and serenity of Hope Farm:

> The many-speckled fowls were pecking about in the farmyard beyond, and the milk-cans glittered with brightness, hung out to sweeten. The court was so full of flowers that they crept out upon the low-covered wall and horse-mount, and were even to be found self-sown upon the turf that bordered the path to the back of the house. I fancied that my Sunday coat was scented for days afterwards by the bushes of sweetbriar and the fraxinella that perfumed the air. (p. 229)

Phillis's life is no idyll, but is rooted in the practical daily tasks of a farmer's daughter: we see her picking peas, peeling apples, mending socks, knitting. She is an intelligent girl who loves studying with her father, with whom she has a great affinity; he is both a farmer and a nonconformist minister, a man of considerable learning, of deep sympathy and love. Holdsworth is able to share in their intellectual pursuits, using his knowledge of Italian to help Phillis translate Dante. Phillis's mother and Paul are simpler people, not widely educated, and thus excluded from many of the interests of the other three; it is perhaps the main deficiency in Phillis's character that she is unaware of her mother's isolation and feelings of inferiority which this has occasioned.

Holdsworth leaves unexpectedly to take up a post in Canada; just before his departure, he admits to Paul that he loves Phillis and hopes to return in perhaps two years and tell her so. It is, however, obvious to the reader that he is more superficial than Phillis, more extrovert, less serious, and that this will be reflected in the quality of his feelings. This turns out to be the case, and it is not long before he writes from Canada telling of his marriage there. Unfortunately, Paul has already told Phillis of Holdsworth's love, to comfort her, as he becomes aware of her deep feelings for his friend. The news of Holdsworth's marriage therefore comes as an even greater shock to her, and results in a brain fever from which she makes a very slow, painful recovery.

We are given some moving insights into the character of Phillis's father, who has never fully accepted the fact that his beloved daughter is no longer a small child: indeed, she is nineteen before she stops wearing childish pinafores. When he learns that Paul has told her of Holdsworth's love, he is enraged:

'So young, so pure from the world! how could you go and talk to such a child, raising hopes, exciting feelings — all to end thus; and best so, even though I saw her poor piteous face look as it did. I can't forgive you, Paul; it was more than wrong — it was wicked — to go and repeat that man's words.' (pp. 307–8)

And when Phillis then upbraids her father for blaming Paul, explaining that she has indeed loved Holdsworth, he is unable to understand:

'Phillis! did we not make you happy here? Have we not loved you enough?... And yet you would have left us, left your home, left your father and your mother, and gone away with this stranger, wandering over the world.' (pp. 308–9)

Although Phillis regains her physical strength, she remains languid, uninterested in the life around her, till the old family servant, Betty, reprimands her:

'If I were you, I'd rise and snuff the moon, sooner than break your father's and your mother's hearts wi' watching and waiting till it pleases you to fight your own way back to cheerfulness. There, I never favoured long preachings, and I've had my say.' (p. 316)

Mrs Gaskell excelled in her portrayals of the outspoken old servant, full of commonsense and ready to give good advice; other examples are Dixon in *North and South* and Kester in *Sylvia's Lovers*, and we have already seen Sally upbraiding Ruth in a manner similar to Betty's.

Phillis does indeed, a day or two after this, show enough strength of character to tell Paul: '"We will go back to the peace of the old days. I know we shall: I can, and I will!"' (p. 317) We admire her determination, but are not totally convinced by it. We must also admire the splendid rural setting and the well-drawn characters in this finely written story and, especially, the portrayal of Phillis's maturing emotions.

The four stories we have just considered illustrate Elizabeth Gaskell's skill in creating credible characters, and in evoking convincingly a particular mood and setting. On the other hand, *My Lady Ludlow* demonstrates her inability on occasions to construct a well-shaped story. She was by no means always successful as a short-story writer, but it is evident, from reading *Lois the Witch* and *Cousin Phillis*, that she could and did master this genre.

8 A Glance into the Past: *Sylvia's Lovers*

> One that loved not wisely but too well.
>
> Shakespeare: *Othello*

Mrs Gaskell set her only historical novel in the 1790s during the period of the Napoleonic Wars. These were characterised by many naval engagements between the French and English, and finding enough sailors to man the ships was a continual problem for England. During the eighteenth century many sailors were, in fact, prisoners drafted from the gaols who, owing to the appalling prison conditions, were often very sickly. This, in conjunction with the insanitary way of life on board ship, resulted in constant epidemics with many fatalities.

The other main and increasingly important source of naval manpower was impressment, particularly of seafaring men. This was carried out by the greatly feared press-gangs, companies of officers and men commissioned to execute warrants on able-bodied men between the ages of eighteen and fifty-five who were liable for service in the fleet:

> For in the great struggle in which England was then involved, the navy was esteemed her safeguard; and men must be had at any price of money or suffering, or of injustice. (p. 249)

The press-gangs were particularly active in ports and on the nearby coastline, where they more easily found likely men. They even extended their activities to ships such as whalers, returning to port after an absence of many months, in order to seize men for service in the navy. This practice was at its height in the 1790s and provided the dramatic backcloth for *Sylvia's Lovers*.

The plot is relatively straightforward: Sylvia, a young girl when the novel opens, is lovely, but somewhat spoilt and wild, a rebel with a strong personality. She falls in love with Charley Kinraid, a successful 'specksioneer' (chief harpooner on a whaling boat), who is a handsome, dashing, charismatic man, and they make a solemn vow to marry. Kinraid is then seized by the press-gang, but is widely thought to have drowned; only Sylvia's cousin, Philip Hepburn, who sees the capture, is aware of the truth. He has always loved Sylvia and decides to conceal his knowledge, believing that Kinraid is fickle and no good for Sylvia, and also, of course, hoping to improve his own chances with her. Her father, Daniel Robson, a passionate man, had himself once worked on a whaling ship, and had been seized by a press-gang. He is particularly enraged by the devious methods being used by a press-gang in Monkshaven, the seaside town (based on Whitby) nearest to his farm at Haytersbank, and he leads a counter-attack to free some men just seized. The result is a near riot, after which he is arrested and eventually hanged for felony. This is disastrous for his wife and daughter; they are no longer able to maintain the farm, and Bell Robson's wits begin to fail. Through all their troubles, Philip is of the greatest help. He is a steady, reliable young man, who has risen from the position of clerk to that of partner in the chief drapers' shop in Monkshaven (based on a shop owned by the Sanders brothers) and is now comfortably off. Sylvia, who has always found him dull and without the glamour she yearns for, agrees to marry him, for she believes that Kinraid is dead, and knows that Philip will provide a comfortable home for her, and more importantly for her mother, to whom both she and Philip are devoted. Three years later, when Sylvia and Philip already have a child, Kinraid returns. The lives of the three main protagonists are now tragically shattered. Kinraid recovers from the blow relatively quickly, but for Philip it is the beginning of long and tortuous wanderings, which end in his return Monkshaven and his death after a reconciliation with Sylvia, who finally realises how headstrong she has been, and how she has underestimated Philip's worth.

What distinguishes this novel from Mrs Gaskell's others is that the three main characters all exhibit a *major* flaw in their personalities. Sylvia, until almost the end of the story, is hard and unforgiving; when she hears that Philip has hidden the truth about Kinraid's disappearance, she vows: '"I'll never forgive yon man, nor live with him as his wife again."' (p. 383) and she reiterates this theme until her reconciliation with Philip on his death-bed. Kinraid is a man unable to experience a lasting and deep love. It is true that he is not as incapable of feeling as his earlier escapades suggest, nor as Philip believes him to be, for he does remain faithful to Sylvia during his years of enforced absence. Philip, in fact, admits with surprise and self-deprecation: '"I niver thought you'd ha' kept true to her!"' (p. 431) However, on finding that he cannot marry Sylvia, Kinraid recovers remarkably quickly, and is soon married to a highly eligible young lady. As Sylvia ruefully remarks: '"Them as one thinks t'most on, forgets one soonest."' (p. 446) She is painfully aware of the contrast between her love and that of Kinraid, whose

> . . . old, passionate love for herself had faded away and vanished utterly: its very existence apparently blotted out of his memory. She had torn up her love for him by the roots, but she felt as if she could never forget that it had been. (p. 451)

The flaw in Philip's character is probably the most serious, and his sufferings in consequence are greater than those of Kinraid or of Sylvia. He tries at first to justify to himself his deliberate duplicity, recalling Kinraid's reputation with women, and also

> . . . deceiving his own conscience by repeating to it the lie that long ere this Kinraid was in all probability dead — killed by either the chances of war or tempestuous sea. (p. 329)

Even before Kinraid's return, however, Philip does not experience the happiness he had expected from marriage with Sylvia. In the first place, he has nightmares about Kinraid's return and, secondly, Sylvia has changed from the wilful, carefree, impetuous young girl he had fallen in love with. The sorrows she has experienced (the loss of Kinraid, her father's execution, her mother's weakened mind) have turned her into a quiet, docile, almost passive woman. She carries out her duties as Philip's wife, but he is well aware that she does not return his love and ' . . . the long-desired happiness was not so delicious and perfect as he had anticipated'. (p. 343)

After Sylvia's passionate renunciation of him, Philip disappears from Monkshaven, and the last hundred pages of the novel are much concerned with his wanderings and sufferings. He enlists in the marines under an assumed name, and ends up in the eastern Mediterranean, where the French are besieging Acre; here, by one of those implausible coincidences which so appealed to Mrs Gaskell, he saves the life of Kinraid, who is lying wounded on the battlefield. Soon after this, Philip himself is badly injured by an explosion on board ship; he is permanently disfigured and so sickly that he is eventually sent back to England and pensioned out of the service. This section of the book, set in an area which Mrs Gaskell had never visited, is not convincing, and weakens the impact of the highly dramatic, passionate story of Sylvia and her two lovers, and of the exploits of the press-gang.

Philip painfully makes his way back to Monkshaven. There is one poignant episode where he finds rest and peace at St Sepulchre's, a hospice for wounded soldiers, but he feels unable to stay there for long, as he is drawn towards Sylvia and his daughter, Bella, though expecting only to see them occasionally and from a distance.

In yet another coincidence, the weak, maimed Philip is on hand to jump in and save Bella when a huge wave washes her over the cliff-side. He is fatally injured, but his action leads to a death-bed reconciliation with Sylvia, during which some of Mrs Gaskell's deeply-held beliefs are emphasised. Philip acknowledges that he has sinned against Sylvia and against God; he explains that his love for Sylvia was wrong:

'I ha' made thee my idol; and if I could live my life o'er again I would love my God more, and thee less; and then I shouldn't ha' sinned this sin against thee.' (p. 495)

Sylvia, on her part, admits that her pitilessness was wicked and has only brought her sorrow. They both freely confess they have wronged each other and, as Philip dies, they pray for forgiveness. It is a fitting conclusion to a story in which there is more passion and tragedy than is usual in Elizabeth Gaskell's work. The final affirmation of true religious belief, an important element throughout the book, is in keeping with her overall attitude.

The first part of the book is convincingly written; the characters are finely drawn and the descriptive writing is full of closely observed, vivid detail. Let us look first at a few of the characters more fully. In Sylvia's eyes, Philip is dull and conventional: he tries to persuade her to buy grey rather than scarlet material for a

St Mary's Church, Whitby, referred to in *Sylvia's Lovers* as
St Nicholas, Monkshaven

The harbour, Whitby, as it is now

(*above*)
Brook Street Unitarian
Chapel, Knutsford
(*right*)
The grave of Elizabeth and
William Gaskell, Brook
Street Unitarian Chapel,
Knutsford

ELIZABETH CLEGHORN GASKELL
BORN SEPTEMBER 29TH 1810
DIED NOVEMBER 12TH 1865

WILLIAM GASKELL
BORN JULY 24TH 1805
DIED JUNE 11TH 1884

cloak, telling her it will wear better; he tries (at her mother's request) to teach her to read and write, but she can see no practical use for this, showing interest only in geography, so that she can find out where Kinraid goes on his whaling trips; at a New Year's Eve party, Philip is reserved and disapproving. But the young Sylvia does not appreciate his sterling, dependable qualities; he is a shrewd businessman, a loyal and trusted employee, a devoted nephew, a tender, thoughtful lover and later husband. He is a man of deep feeling, which is evident in his love for Sylvia and his jealousy of Kinraid, but his natural reserve and his puritanical outlook result in the suppression of these feelings. He develops at last into a more sensitive and understanding man, aware of his own shortcomings.

Sylvia inherits much of her passion and waywardness from her father. Daniel Robson is an outspoken man with a zest for life; he is highly emotional and obsessed by the activities of the press-gang, which he regards as his natural enemy. His devotion to his wife and daughter is evident, in spite of outbursts of bad temper and abusiveness. He, like his daughter, is attracted by Kinraid's carefree courage and spirit of adventure, and is, therefore, in favour of Sylvia's engagement to him, preferring him to Philip for reasons similar to hers. He is portrayed as a warm-hearted man, caught up in events more complex than he can understand, fundamentally kindly, but led into deep trouble by his impetuousness.

Many of the minor characters are also well-drawn. For example, Molly Corney, Sylvia's girlhood friend, is a vulgar, outspoken young woman, whose coarseness is reminiscent of Sally Leadbitter's in *Mary Barton*. Molly leaves Monkshaven after her marriage to a much older man, a comfortably-off shopkeeper, and it is a measure of Sylvia's development that subsequently she finds Molly patronising, selfish and tactless. Referring to Daniel Robson's death, Molly says:

'Such an end for a decent man to come to! Many a one come an' called on me o' purpose to hear all I could tell 'em about him!'
'Please don't speak on it!' said Sylvia, trembling all over. (p. 436)

She continues in the same insensitive way to tell Sylvia that: '"But to give t' devil his due, it were good i' Hepburn to marry thee, and so soon after there was a' that talk about thy feyther."' (p. 436)

Kester, the farm-labourer employed by Daniel Robson, is another finely portrayed character. He is an old man with a deep loyalty to the Robsons; this is beautifully evoked when he pays a farewell visit to Daniel awaiting execution. None of Daniel's attempts at light-hearted joking, we are told,

> ... could make Kester smile, or do anything except groan in but a heart-broken sort of fashion, and presently the talk had become more suitable to the occasion, Daniel being up to the last the more composed of the two; for Kester, when turned out of the condemned cell, fairly broke down into the heavy sobbing he had never thought to sob again on earth. (p. 316)

He is particularly attached to Sylvia, who often works with him on the farm, and he claims the privilege of an old friend to give her a forthright opinion; for example, he supports her attachment to Kinraid, even after the latter has supposedly drowned, and when she tells him that she is thinking of marrying Philip, he offers, in preference, to try and support her and her mother himself:

> 'But dunnot go and marry a man as thou's noane taken wi', and another as is most like for t' be dead, but who, mebbe, is alive, havin' a pull on thy heart.' (p. 325)

But after her marriage he remains a faithful friend to whom Sylvia can turn for support. He too, like Sylvia, finally realises Philip's worth, and as Philip dies, once more sobs bitterly.

Although *Sylvia's Lovers* was not published until 1863, Mrs Gaskell had begun to write it at the end of 1859, after spending a short holiday in Whitby with two of her daughters, thus gaining first-hand knowledge of the area. Her pleasure in it is evident from the many sensitive and accurate pictures she gives us of Monkshaven and its surroundings, and of the occupations of the inhabitants. In the opening chapter, as is often her practice, she paints the main features of the countryside with broad strokes, stressing the contrast between the open moorland and the sheltered valleys:

> . . . high above the level of the sea towered the purple crags, whose summits were crowned with greensward that stole down the sides of the scaur a little way in grassy veins. Here and there a brook forced its way from the heights down to the sea, making its channel into a valley more or less broad in long process of time. And in the moorland hollows, as in these valleys, trees and underwood grew and flourished; so that, while on the bare swells of the high land you shivered at the waste desolation of the scenery, when you dropped into these wooded 'bottoms' you were charmed with the nestling shelter which they gave. (p. 3)

Then, in the next chapter, as Sylvia and Molly approach Monkshaven to sell their farm produce, the detail is added: how the river was 'swelling and chaffing', and the picture of the town which greeted the girls:

> The red and fluted tiles of the gabled houses rose in crowded irregularity on one side of the river, while the newer suburb was built in more orderly and less picturesque fashion on the opposite cliff. (p. 18)

It is to be expected that in a story concerned with seafaring men, the sea itself will form an important background to much of the action, and there are some stirring descriptions of the sea's powerful strength, thundering noise and relentless force:

> Sylvia heard the sound of the passionate rush and rebound of many waters, like the shock of mighty guns, whenever the other sound of the blustering gusty wind was lulled for an instant. (p. 369)

There are also some vivid descriptions of weather, so that we actually feel surrounded by damp mist, or experience the contrast between the cold, dark winter's night and the warmth and light of the farmhouse at Haytersbank, or enjoy the pleasant warmth of a May evening with its spring sights and sounds. We are also aware of the day-to-day texture of the lives of the characters, but especially of Sylvia's life, of her household duties or her work on the farm:

> Sylvia sat in the house-place, her back to the long low window, in order to have all the light the afternoon hour afforded for her work. A basket of her father's unmended stockings was on the little round table beside her, and one was on her left hand, which she supposed herself to be mending. (p. 193)

The strength of *Sylvia's Lovers* lies in the detailed, lively pictures we are given of the characters, their homely occupations, their surroundings and their very human qualities and failings; it loses its power when Mrs Gaskell moves the setting and action to an environment unfamiliar to her. In the concluding chapter, she indeed stresses the importance of forgiveness, in which she deeply believed; still, the overall effect of the last part of the novel is laboured and drawn out.

9 Mature Accomplishment: *Wives and Daughters*

Marriage is a very fine institution; no family should be without one.
Anon.

Wives and Daughters is set in Hollingford which, like Cranford, is probably modelled on Knutsford,[1] but Elizabeth Gaskell's skill as a writer had matured since she wrote *Cranford* and we are, as a result, presented with a more complex and fully developed society than in the earlier book. We are shown the relationships, not only among its inhabitants, but also between them and the local squire's family, who live seven miles away in Hamley, and between them and the local aristocracy, Lord and Lady Cumnor and their family, whose country seat, Cumnor Towers, is situated just outside Hollingford. The novel was published in monthly instalments in the *Cornhill Magazine* from August 1864. The final instalment, due to be published in January 1866, had not been written when Mrs Gaskell died suddenly in November 1865, although she had made an outline of its contents.

The story centres round the second marriage of Mr Gibson, the local doctor. As a widower, he is deeply concerned about the problems of bringing up his daughter, Molly, the heroine of the story, without the influence and protection of a mother. He therefore proposes rather precipitately to a widow, Mrs Kirkpatrick, a former governess of the Cumnors, who refer to her by her maiden name, Clare. Since the death of her husband, she has had a hard struggle to keep herself and her daughter, running an unsuccessful small school, so she is only too ready to accept such an eligible man, her first reaction to his proposal being: ' . . . it was such a wonderful relief to feel that she need not struggle any more for a livelihood'. (p. 140) Molly, who has had a very close relationship with her father, is devastated by his news: 'It was if the piece of solid ground on which she stood had broken from the shore, and she was drifting out to the infinite sea alone'. (p. 145) She is slightly reconciled to the idea by the thought of having a sister of her own age, Cynthia Kirkpatrick, who at the time of the wedding is at school in Boulogne.

The relationship between these four people is largely determined by their characters. Mr Gibson, a forthright, honest man, soon realises that his second wife is a superficial, rather silly woman, incapable of serious thought or of distinguishing clearly between right and wrong. Nevertheless, he accepts that he must make the best of this self-imposed situation, and does not allow himself to dwell on his unfortunate choice of a wife. Molly who, like her father, is completely straightforward and truthful, soon realises that her stepmother has very different standards. However, loyalty to her father and a strong desire to secure his peace of mind result in her trying hard to conform to her stepmother's aspirations to gentility; she even reluctantly agrees to call her 'mamma'. Cynthia is a much more complex character. As a young girl she was neglected by her mother, who resented her. Her attitude towards her mother is therefore ambivalent; although in company and in the presence of Mr Gibson, of whom she is a little afraid, she behaves properly, she is frequently contemptuous of her mother, exploiting her weaknesses and foibles. She longs to be loved and admired, and values especially the good opinion of Mr Gibson and of Molly. However, she tends to be secretive, and Molly, although she loves Cynthia dearly, finds that her unpredictable moods are hard to understand.

Cynthia's passionate desire for admiration leads her into various romantic relationships, around which much of the story revolves. There is her secret engagement to Lord Cumnor's land-agent, Mr Preston, formed when she was only sixteen; she comes to regret this involvement bitterly, but the threat of blackmail (because of some letters she had written to him) prevents her from ending the relationship. Molly eventually chances on the truth and, acting in a courageous, determined manner, extricates Cynthia from this awkward situation. Cynthia has meanwhile become engaged to Squire Hamley's younger son, Roger. He is a brilliant scientist, whose attentions flatter Cynthia but, as she is well aware, she is incapable of deep feeling, and is unable to return Roger's love. During his absence on a long, dangerous scientific mission in Africa, she shows little interest in his letters, whilst Molly, who greatly admires and is devoted to Roger, laps up every detail of his life that she can acquire. During Cynthia's engagement to Roger (which on her insistence is known only to their immediate families), she flirts so openly that she attracts a proposal from a former pupil of Mr Gibson's, and brings on herself a severe reprimand from her stepfather. She finds it difficult to understand what she has done wrong, and explains to Molly: '"I've never lived with people with such a high standard of conduct before; and I don't quite know how to behave."' (p. 456) We are told that she also responds with pleasure to the attentions of a rich young London lawyer, Mr Henderson, and she finally breaks off her engagement to Roger and accepts Mr Henderson, saying of Roger: '"I don't like people of deep feelings. . . . They don't suit me."' (p. 656)

Roger, recovering relatively quickly from being jilted, begins to appreciate Molly's admirable qualities, and acknowledges his new-found love for her to Mr Gibson. However, as he is about to return to Africa to complete his assignment, he agrees not to declare his love until he comes home again. It is the scene which would have included the open acknowledgement of this love, and of Molly's response, that Mrs Gaskell never wrote.

There is an interesting sub-plot involving mainly Squire Hamley and his elder son, Osborne, who has not fulfilled his early academic promise, and is a great disappointment to his father. There are many misunderstandings between them, of which the root cause is lack of openness. The most obvious example is Osborne's secret marriage to a young French girl, a Catholic, formerly a servant. Knowing his father's aversion to all aspects of his wife's background, Osborne is never able to confide in him, and it is only after Osborne's early death that Squire Hamley finds out about his son's wife and child.

Indeed, the main didactic element in *Wives and Daughters* (as in so much of Mrs Gaskell's writing) concerns the importance of honesty, openness and integrity, and the harmful results of deviousness, secrecy and dishonourable behaviour. An outstanding example occurs when Mrs Gibson eavesdrops on a medical discussion between her husband and a specialist on Osborne Hamley's possibly fatal illness. Because of what she learns, Mrs Gibson changes her attitude to the Hamley brothers. Previously she has greatly favoured Osborne's visits, believing him to be Squire Hamley's heir and therefore a desirable son-in-law. On the other hand, she has thought of Roger as uncouth and boorish, and her behaviour towards him has bordered on the uncivil. However, if Osborne is fatally ill, the younger son immediately becomes in her eyes a more attractive suitor, and so she starts to encourage Roger's visits and to approve of his interest in Cynthia. When Mr Gibson discovers his wife's duplicity, he tries to make her see how wrongly she has behaved, but she is incapable of understanding what she has done wrong, and is at a loss when Mr Gibson's manner towards her becomes more bitter and sarcastic. She responds in the superficial manner typical of her:

> 'I think dear papa seems a little put out today; we must see that he has a dinner that he likes when he comes home. I have often perceived that everything depends on making a man comfortable in his own house.' (pp. 457–8)

The secrecy surrounding Cynthia's engagement to Mr Preston is also shown to have many harmful effects, the most damaging of which involves Molly. During her efforts to release Cynthia, she has to meet Mr Preston privately, and by ill luck she is seen on each occasion. The news spreads quickly, with the result that Molly is condemned as an improper young lady who has lost her good name. It takes the open support and trust of Lady Harriet, Lord Cumnor's daughter, to still the rumours.

Another complication resulting from Cynthia's involvement with Mr Preston is her insistence on her engagement to Roger remaining secret. It is made clear throughout that Mr Gibson, who cannot understand the reason for this, strongly disapproves of such mysteries and concealment. This is an attitude shared by Roger, who wishes his brother would disclose his own marriage to their father, and by Molly who by chance is privy to that secret also:

> . . . there was a sense of concealment and uncertainty about it all; and her honest straightforward father, her quiet life at Hollingford, which, even with all its drawbacks, was above-board, and where everybody knew what everybody was doing, seemed secure and pleasant in comparison. (p. 249)

Thus, the characters whose attitudes Mrs Gaskell most strongly approves of are united in condemning underhand behaviour.

It is a great tribute to Mrs Gaskell's skill as a mature writer that the underlying seriousness of her strong moral stand on overt, candid behaviour is presented with a light, humorous touch, mainly through the words and actions of the characters, without the use of a narrator and with little authorial comment, both of which she used in earlier works. Her manner of describing Mrs Gibson's reactions, in particular, demonstrates her effective use of gentle irony. For example, on learning from Lady Cumnor of Cynthia's former engagement to Mr Preston, she upbraids her daughter, but skirts around the error of deceit, which she obviously does not appreciate:

> 'You've entangled yourself with him, and you've done something of the sort with Mr Preston, and got yourself into such an imbroglio' (Mrs Gibson could not have said 'mess' for the world, although the word was present to her mind), 'that when a really eligible person comes forward — handsome, agreeable, and quite the gentleman — and a good private fortune into the bargain, you have to refuse him. You'll end as an old maid, Cynthia, and it will break my heart.' (p. 595)

Mrs Gibson's lack of self-awareness, another clear failing, is again and again made evident. She is jealous of her particular relationship with the Cumnor family, and dislikes especially Lady Harriet's obvious fondness for Molly. At the local charity ball, she resents any conversation Lady Harriet has with Molly or with other Hollingford residents, explaining that: '"If there is one thing I hate more than another, it is the trying to make out an intimacy with great people."' (p. 336) This occurs shortly after a delightful episode at the Towers, in which Mrs Gibson is largely ignored, but which she retails to her family implying that she was the centre of the Cumnor family's attention.

The justification for the sub-title of *Wives and Daughters*, 'An Everyday Story', is apparent in the texture of the novel; it is largely concerned with everyday relationships between characters, with the everyday events which make up their lives, and with the effects on them of birth, love, marriage and death. We learn of the life of a busy doctor with a demanding practice which brings him into contact with all classes of society, of the constant pressure imposed by his work, his rushed meals, his inability to participate without interruption in social engagements. We learn of the problems faced by a landowner and farmer, Squire Hamley, struggling to find sufficient money for draining and reclaiming some of his land, and of the consequences for him and his labourers when he is unable to do so. We learn of the everyday difficulties experienced by Mrs Gibson before her second marriage, as she struggles to make ends meet; how her clothes were in tints of violet and grey, supposedly in half-mourning for the late Mr Kirkpatrick, but: 'in reality because it was both lady-like and economical', (p. 129) and of how she did not follow the accepted custom and keep her head covered: 'partly because the washing of caps is expensive.' (p. 129) We learn more of everyday family life than from any other of Mrs Gaskell's works: of domestic arrangements, including the decorating and furnishing of the Gibson home, even of their meal-times, of how the table should be set, of the food they eat:

'I shouldn't like to think of your father eating cheese; it's such a strong-smelling, coarse kind of thing. We must get him a cook who can toss him up an omelette, or something elegant. Cheese is only fit for the kitchen.' (p. 162)

There are frequent references to how Mrs Gibson and her daughters fill their day: Mrs Gibson: 'at her everlasting worsted-work frame' (p. 262), Cynthia, 'a capital workwoman' (p. 255) making pretty bonnets from odd bits of ribbon and gauze, Molly conscientiously practising the piano, engaging in plain sewing or reading avidly, (especially books recommended by Roger.)

Indeed, *Wives and Daughters* provides a wealth of material about the lives of middle-class families of the period, for it is of them that Mrs Gaskell writes with such obvious authority and with whom she largely identifies. Although *Wives and Daughters* is set in the period forty years before it was written,[2] most of the features of everyday life of the middle-class had not substantially altered, and, although class relationships were changing, it was a slow process. In any case, the society described reflects the Knutsford of the earlier period when Elizabeth Gaskell was living there. She especially enjoys satirising snobbery and prejudice, and the charity ball, where the assembled company comes from many strata of society, provides an excellent occasion for her gentle irony. The highlight of the evening is to be the arrival of the party from Cumnor Towers, accompanied by their guest, the duchess of Menteith, but their late appearance gives rise to many complaints: 'Everyone of any pretensions to gentility was painfully affected by the absence of the family from the Towers'; whilst 'it was only the butchers and bakers and candlestickmakers who rather enjoyed the absence of restraint, and were happy and hilarious', (p. 332) 'The punctual plebeians of Hollingford' are indeed the only ones not affected by the 'aristocratic ozone being absent from the atmosphere'. (p. 327) When the aristocrats do finally arrive, the anticlimax is highly disagreeable:

> . . . in came Lord Cumnor in his state dress, with a fat middle-aged woman on his arm; she was dressed almost like a girl — in a sprigged muslin, with natural flowers in her hair, but not a vestige of a jewel or a diamond. Yet it must be the duchess; but what was a duchess without diamonds? — and in a dress which Farmer Hodson's daughter might have worn! (p. 332)

One cannot help comparing such descriptions with those of Jane Austen; the resemblances are even more marked than those previously noted between *North and South* and *Pride and Prejudice*. Miss Hopkins, in drawing attention to some of the similarities between Elizabeth Gaskell and Jane Austen, writes:

> *Wives and Daughters* again recalls Miss Austen in taking much the same humorous view of the world that prevails in her novels. Yet there is a difference, too. While the book is shot through with irony and satire, the fun-poking is not quite so sharp as Miss Austen's. But it is sharper than anywhere else in Mrs Gaskell.[3]

Also like Jane Austen, Mrs Gaskell is deeply concerned with the relationship between love and marriage. Consider the marriages of the Gibsons in *Wives and Daughters* and of the Bennets in *Pride and Prejudice*: in both cases, the husband is an intelligent man of integrity, whilst the wife is fatuous and vain; in neither case is there real love between the partners, for the Gibsons' marriage is based on expediency, whilst Mr Bennet had been ' . . . captivated by youth and beauty', and ' . . . had married a woman whose weak understanding and illiberal mind had very early in their marriage put an end to all real affection for her'.[4] Both marriages are portrayed as unsatisfactory because they are not based on mutual love and esteem.

In *Wives and Daughters*, an interesting contrast is provided between the marriages of the Gibsons and the Hamleys, who also have little in common. Mrs Hamley, ' . . . a delicate fine London lady' (p. 73), is, by the time we meet her, a chronic invalid. We see her only in the last stages of her life, an unselfish woman of understanding and sympathy. In contrast to the squire, she is a widely-read woman of taste and refinement, but she loves her husband sufficiently to sacrifice her pleasure in educated society, in which he cannot share. He, in his turn, loves her even more for this sacrifice. So, in spite of their markedly different characters, the Hamleys' marriage is a good one, because it is based on deep love. The loss to the whole family on the death of Mrs Hamley is finely described:

> Her husband, who was often restless and angry from one cause or another, always came to her to be smoothed down and put right. He was conscious of her pleasant influence over him, and became at peace with himself when in her presence; just as a child is at ease when with someone who is both firm and gentle. But the keystone of the family arch was gone, and the stones of which it was composed began to fall apart. (pp. 285–6)

In her novels, Elizabeth Gaskell frequently delineates a close father-daughter relationship; obvious examples are those between John and Mary Barton, Mr Hale and Margaret, Daniel and Sylvia Robson, and Mr Gibson and Molly. In each case, it is a loving relationship, in which the daughter loyally supports her father, even when (as in the cases of John Barton and Daniel Robson) he is guilty of a criminal act. The relationship is portrayed as uncomplicated, almost without tension, virtually ideal. We also see Margaret Hale and Sylvia Robson as daughters devoted to their mothers, but in neither case is the relationship central to the novel, or even deeply considered. It is only in *Wives and Daughters* that Elizabeth Gaskell explores more fully the mother–daughter relationship, particularly that between Mrs Gibson and Cynthia. The interplay and tensions between them, the layers of meaning in many of their exchanges (for example, those concerning Mr Preston), are realistically portrayed, and an evident awareness of the complexities of this relationship suggests that Mrs Gaskell was drawing on her own experience. We hear of Mrs Gibson ' . . .unconscious of any satire in Cynthia's speech', yet ' . . .fluttered and annoyed as she usually was with the Lilliputian darts Cynthia flung at her'. (p. 401) We hear of Cynthia's assumed indifference ' . . . to countervene Mrs Gibson's affectation and false sentiment'. (p. 443) Cynthia clearly believes that her unsatisfactory relationship with her mother is due to her upbringing: '"Oh, how good you are, Molly! I wonder, if I had been brought up like you, whether I should have been as good. But I've been tossed about so."' (p. 372) There is, however, no suggestion that Elizabeth Gaskell's relationship with her daughters was other than a loving, caring one, but in all such situations tensions exist, and her experience of these lends authenticity to the portrayal of the Mrs Gibson–Cynthia relationship.

In his introduction to the Penguin edition, Laurence Lerner describes *Wives and Daughters* as: ' . . . the most under-rated novel in English'. (p. 27) We are presented with a greatly extended *Cranford*; there are, it is true, the Miss Brownings, Mrs Goodenough, Mrs Dawes and other minor characters, who have their parallels in *Cranford*, but the triumph of *Wives and Daughters* lies in the credible drawing of many varied, often complex, characters from so many strata of society, and of the convincing development of their relationships. We are presented with a broad canvas, handled with skill, which leaves us with a delightful impression of a many-faceted community, described with a light, sure and humorous touch.

Notes

1. See Angus Easson, *Elizabeth Gaskell*, Routledge & Kegan Paul, London, 1979, p. 187. He considers Hollingford may be situated in Warwickshire.
2. This point is referred to in L. 550.
3. Hopkins, *Elizabeth Gaskell, Her Life and Work*, p. 279.
4. *Pride and Prejudice*, chap. 42.

10 Retrospect

> Few people have ever more deserved to be remembered.
>
> Anon.[1]

There is no contradiction between the principles and standards which Elizabeth Gaskell followed in her own life and those which she extolled in her writing.

The importance which she attached to a close-knit, caring family, and to the woman's role in promoting this, is evident from what we know of her own life, from the subject-matter and underlying concern of many of her letters, and from the presentation of family life in her stories. Two examples taken from her first and her last novel will serve to illustrate this latter point: *Mary Barton* opens happily with two families enjoying an outing; during the hard, tragic events of the story, both families break up, but it is on a happy family note that the novel ends. It is carried beyond the marriage of Jem and Mary to their life in Canada with Jem's mother and with their first-born child. In *Wives and Daughters* we learn of the lives of three families: that of the Cumnors is happy, because (as in the case of the Hamleys) it is founded on a happy marriage; that of the Hamleys is also good until, on Mrs Hamley's death, it disintegrates; that of the Gibsons, however unsatisfactory, is more stable than their individual lives before they married. The general emphasis is on the benefits conferred by a complete, well-established family.

It is also clear from her own life and from the values emphasised in her writing that religion was of paramount importance to Elizabeth Gaskell; her religion was above all a caring one, in which empathy for the weak, the disadvantaged and the persecuted was uppermost. She did not, for example, spare herself in helping those who were suffering during the cotton famine of 1861–3. The cause of this was the American Civil War, which resulted in the cutting off of supplies of raw cotton to the Lancashire mills and, as a consequence, half a million people became unemployed and destitute. Several of her letters refer to the efforts which she and her family made to help these people:

Last autumn & winter was *such* hard work — we were often off at nine, — not to come home till 7, or ½ past, too worn out to eat or do anything but go to bed. The one thought ran thro' all our talk almost like a disease. (L. 526)

She also depicted with humanity and understanding many characters who were victims of circumstance: a few examples are Alice Wilson and Esther, Ruth, Lois, Bessy Higgins and Philip Hepburn.

Mrs Gaskell's main impact has, of course, been through her writing. Her gift as a story-teller is indisputable; it was with good reason that Dickens referred to her as 'My dear Scheherazade'. Her work is, in the main, didactic, based on her strong moral attitude. She considered honesty, truthfulness and integrity as the supreme virtues. She was a forthright, sincere, honest writer whose wide reading, interest in social problems and awareness of prevailing new ideas are reflected in her writing. It must be admitted that there is sometimes a lack of structure, so that her stories ramble on, and there is on occasion a cloying sentimentality and an unconvincing use of coincidence. However, we are continually rewarded by the finely-observed detail which characterises her descriptions of people and of scenes, both indoor and outdoor, and which lifts much of her writing from the commonplace to the first-rate.

Elizabeth Gaskell embodied in her work the pre-eminent, conventional attitudes of the Victorian middle-class: the overriding importance of the family, the central position of religion as the mainspring of moral and humanitarian values, the belief in her duty to ameliorate the lot of the disadvantaged and the conviction that this could be achieved through the goodwill, co-operation and understanding of all concerned.

She shared these attitudes and concerns with many contemporary novelists; this was indeed a time when the novel was a proliferating and increasingly important art form. Dickens, Thackeray, the Brontë sisters, George Eliot, Trollope, George Meredith, Disraeli, Kingsley and Wilkie Collins were amongst those publishing novels at the same time as Elizabeth Gaskell. Whilst some of these, perhaps most outstandingly Dickens, Charlotte and Emily Brontë and George Eliot, have unhesitatingly been accorded a position of supremacy, there has been a tendency to relegate Elizabeth Gaskell to a minor role, as a writer merely of social criticism in novel form; it has been implied that *Cranford* was a happy, albeit minor, masterpiece, of a different stature from her other novels, although she has been accorded full recognition for her outstanding biography of Charlotte Brontë.

Where then should we place her in relation to her contemporaries? Is the position of minor importance, which she has so often been accorded, justifiable? It must be admitted that she does not possess the ingenuity, exuberance or range of Dickens, nor the deep perception and delicate control of language of George Eliot; she never rises to the heights of dramatic poetry of Emily Brontë's *Wuthering Heights* (but this work stands uniquely apart from all other contemporary fiction). Elizabeth Gaskell did, however, develop into a mature, accomplished writer; the success of *Cranford* may be considered to have done her a disservice, for it has tended to overshadow much of her writing, which is perceptive, sensitive and creative. For too long, she has been under-rated; she deserves to be placed among the important, rather than the minor, novelists of her period. Her capacity for moral analysis and for finely observed nuances of feeling should enable her to take her place alongside the other outstanding contemporary women novelists: George Eliot and Charlotte and Emily Brontë.

With the memory of *Wives and Daughters*, her last and greatest work, uppermost, it is her sense of humour and of the ridiculous, her use of irony tempered with kindness and sympathy, her vitality and obvious enjoyment of her world, which leave a lasting impression on the reader.

Notes

1. Quoted in an article by Mrs Richmond Ritchie, referring to Mrs Gaskell, in the *Cornhill Magazine*, December 1906.

Brief Chronology

1810	29 Sept.	Elizabeth Cleghorn Stevenson born in Chelsea.
1811		Mother died. To Knutsford (Aunt Lumb).
1825–7		Avonbank School.
1828		Brother John disappeared at sea.
1829		Father died.
1832		Married William Gaskell. Settled in Manchester.
1833		Daughter still-born.
1834		Marianne born.
1837		Margaret Emily (Meta) born.
1837		Aunt Lumb died.
1840		'Clopton House' published in *Visits to Remarkable Places*.
1842		Florence Elizabeth (Flossy) born.
1844		William (only son) born.
1845		William died.
1846		Julia Bradford born.
1848		*Mary Barton* published (Chapman & Hall).
1849		Moved to Plymouth Grove, Manchester.
1850		First met Charlotte Brontë.
1851	Dec. (to)	*Cranford* published in *Household Words*.
1853	May	
1853		*Ruth* published (Chapman & Hall).
1855	Sept. (to)	*North and South* published in *Household*
1856	Jan.	*Words*.
1857		*Life of Charlotte Brontë* published (Smith, Elder).
1864		*Sylvia's Lovers* published (Smith, Elder).
1864	Aug. (to)	*Wives and Daughters* published in *Cornhill Magazine*.
1865	12 Nov.	Died at Alton, Hampshire. Buried at Brook Street Unitarian Chapel, Knutsford.
1884		William Gaskell died; buried beside his wife.

Select Bibliography

Works by Elizabeth Gaskell

In order to assist readers I have, where possible, used easily accessible and reasonably priced editions of Elizabeth Gaskell's work; in addition, these all have the bonus of a good introduction.

Page references are to the following editions:

Mary Barton, Penguin English Library (PEL), Harmondsworth, 1970

Cranford/Cousin Phillis, PEL, Harmondsworth, 1976

The Life of Charlotte Brontë, PEL, Harmondsworth, 1975

North and South, PEL, Harmondsworth, 1970

Wives and Daughters, PEL, Harmondsworth, 1969

Ruth, Everyman's Library, Dent, London, 1967

Sylvia's Lovers, World's Classics (WC), OUP, Oxford, 1982

'Half a Life-Time Ago' and 'Lois the Witch', in *Cousin Phillis and Other Tales*, WC, OUP, Oxford, 1981

My Lady Ludlow and Other Tales, Knutsford Edition, vol. 5, John Murray, London, 1919–20

The Letters of Mrs Gaskell, A. Pollard and J. A. V. Chapple (eds.), MUP, Manchester, 1966

Background Reading

Allott, Miriam, *Elizabeth Gaskell* (*Writers and their Work*, no. 124), Longman Group, London, 1950.

Beer, Patricia, *Reader, I Married Him*, Macmillan, London, 1974.

Cecil, David, *Early Victorian Novelists*, Constable, London, 1934.

Chapple, J. A. V., and Arthur Pollard (eds.), *The Letters of Mrs Gaskell*, MUP, Manchester, 1966.

Chapple, J. A. V., assisted by J. G. Sharps, *Elizabeth Gaskell, A Portrait in Letters*, MUP, Manchester, 1980.

Duthie, Enid L., *The Themes of Elizabeth Gaskell*, Macmillan, London, 1980.

Easson, Angus, *Elizabeth Gaskell*, Routledge & Kegan Paul, London, 1979.

Ffrench, Yvonne, *Mrs Gaskell*, Home & Van Thal, London, 1949.

Gérin, Winifred, *Elizabeth Gaskell: A Biography*, OUP, Oxford, 1976.

Hopkins, A. B., *Elizabeth Gaskell: Her Life and Work*, John Lehmann, London, 1952.

McVeagh, John, *Elizabeth Gaskell (Profiles in Literature)*, Routledge & Kegan Paul, London, 1970.

Pollard, Arthur, *Mrs Gaskell, Novelist and Biographer*, MUP, Manchester, 1965.

Sharps, J. G., *Mrs Gaskell's Observation and Invention*, Linden Press, Fontwell, Sussex, 1970.

Tillotson, Kathleen, *Novels of the Eighteen-Forties*, Clarendon Press, Oxford, 1954 (Oxford Paperbacks, 1961).

Whitfield, A. Stanton, *Mrs Gaskell: Her Life and Work*, Routledge & Sons, London, 1929.

Williams, Raymond, *Culture and Society 1780–1950*, Chatto & Windus, London, 1958, (Penguin, Harmondsworth, 1961).

Wright, Edgar, *Mrs Gaskell, A Basis for Reassessment*, OUP, Oxford, 1965.

Index